MW01121962

Pastoral Practice

① How far is counseling from Teaching? All I can see is the Venue maybe different.

Pastoral Practice

Books 3 and 4
of the *Regula Pastoralis* by

SAINT GREGORY THE GREAT

in an English version by
John Leinenweber

TRINITY PRESS INTERNATIONAL
Harrisburg, Pennsylvania

TRINITY PRESS INTERNATIONAL, P.O. Box 1321, Harrisburg, PA 17112

Trinity Press International is a division of the Morehouse Group.

Library of Congress Cataloging-in-Publication Data

Gregory I. Pope, ca. 540–604.
    [Regula pastoralis. Books 3–4. English]
    Pastoral practice : books 3 and 4 of the Regula pastoralis / by Gregory the Great ; in an English version by John Leinenweber.
        p. cm.
    Includes bibliographical references.
    ISBN 1-56338-237-7
    1. Pastoral theology—Early works to 1800. I. Leinenweber, John. II. Title.
BR65.G53R4413   1998
253—dc21   97-45169
                                          CIP

98 99 00 01 02 03   10 9 8 7 6 5 4 3 2 1

To

BISHOP FRANK T. GRISWOLD

pastor and friend

Contents

Introduction

SAINT GREGORY THE GREAT'S treatise on pastoral care, his *Regula Pastoralis*, was a best-seller, so to call it, for many hundreds of years. Gregory was one of the most influential writers of western Europe between the sixth and the sixteenth centuries, not because of his profundity but because of his popularity. His homilies on passages from the gospel, his moral lessons drawn loosely from the book of Job, his interpretations of Ezekiel, Kings, and the Song of Songs, his collection of miracle stories—the *Dialogues*, the second book of which is a life of Saint Benedict—were popular everywhere. The papal register of Gregory's letters provides a unique account of the early medieval papacy at work. *The Regula Pastoralis*, written in 591, spread quickly throughout Europe; at the end of the ninth century Alfred the Great had a translation into Old English made for use in his realm; it was translated into Old French in the thirteenth century, into Italian in the fourteenth, and into Spanish in the sixteenth.

Gregory knew something about power and authority. He was directly descended from one pope, and closely related to another—in contemporary terms, think of relationships to presidents of the United States. While still a young man he was made prefect of the city of Rome—think "mayor of New York City." In about 575 he resigned this position and turned his family home on the Coelian Hill into a monastery dedicated to Saint Andrew. After only a few years of monastic life in the monastery he had founded he was called out to become the pope's ambassador to Constantinople, the imperial capital—imagine the American ambassador to England or to Russia earlier in this century when there was still some uncertainty as to which was the major power. There he continued to live as a monk. After his return to Rome and to Saint Andrew's, Pope Pelagius II chose him as his deacon, his secretary of health, education, and welfare, so to speak. In 590, when the pope died of the plague that followed a flooding of the Tiber, the electors—clergy, nobles, and people of Rome—chose Gregory as his successor. He initially tried to resist his election, writing to the emperor to ask him to refuse his consent. His letter was intercepted, however, and when the imperial confirmation came he bowed to God's will and was consecrated pope on September 3, 590. Despite his regret that so active a ministry had been forced upon him, and his poor health, he served with great effectiveness until his death on March 12, 604.

The *Regula Pastoralis* was one of the first products of his papacy. In a dedicatory letter he explained that he was responding to a request to explain his reluctance to undertake the episcopal office. Part 1 (not included in this volume) stresses the difficulties and responsibilties of the pastoral office. In the troubled circumstances of the time—Rome was being afflicted with enormous political and natural disasters—bishops were becoming in effect civil as well as religious leaders, and as a result the office was attracting men for the wrong reasons. In part 2 (also omitted) Gregory describes the ideal bishop, stressing that his life must be virtuous to accord with his teaching.

In part 3, which makes up the bulk of this present volume, Gregory advises bishops who have come to their position for the right reason, and who live in accord with their profession, on how they ought to counsel the many kinds of persons for whom they bear pastoral responsibility.

Gregory's principle in this (as expressed in chapter 24) is *juxta uniuscuiusque qualitatem,* "in accordance with each one's character." He comments at varying length on thirty-six pairs of qualities. The chapter titles in this volume, which are my abbreviations of those in the Latin text, indicate the kinds of people he is describing. In a very short part 4, included here as the epilogue, Gregory calls on pastors to know themselves.

Jeffrey Richards, who has written a study of Gregory's life and times making ample use of the register of letters, comments:

> By temperament Gregory was a conservative, an authoritarian and a legalist, an old fashioned Roman of the best kind, public servant and paterfamilias. This image is stamped on everything he did, but more subtly it reveals the deep intertwining of *Christianitas and Romanitas...* Unquestionably, however, the single factor which dominated and shaped every aspect of his thought on matters social, political, thelogical and ecclesiastical was the imminence of the end of the world.[1]

This remark may serve to warn readers that they will not find Gregory either nondirective or nonjudgmental. He believed that in view of the imminent judgment human behavior mattered.

Another quotation from Richards may provide further help in understanding Gregory. Of a peace treaty between the Lombards and the Empire he says:

> This became the major diplomatic aim of [Gregory's] pontificate. His reasons for wanting peace blended all the aspects of his complex character: a deeply felt Christian desire to put an end to misery and suffering,

---

1. Jeffrey Richards, *Consul of God* (Boston: Routledge & Kegan Paul, 1980), pp. 50, 52.

a patriotic wish to give the Empire a breathing space for retrenchment, and an estate owner's clear realization that all this turmoil and destruction was bad for business.[2]

These aspects of his character are revealed in his ability to blend both moral and spiritual direction in his counseling.

While acknowledging Gregory's influence in moral and ascetical theology, ecclesiastical and civil administration, monasticism, evangelization, social welfare, and liturgy, it seems that we must deny him one element of his renown. Of the religious chants customarily associated with his name, Richards remarks that if "any Gregory should be credited with sacramentary and antiphonary it is Gregory II."[3]

Gregory's intention in writing the *Regula Pastoralis* was to counsel bishops, for whom he felt pastoral responsibility. I have at times made tendentious translations in an effort to broaden the range of people who may be able to take his words as addressed to them. Few people do not have influence of some kind over someone—bishops, yes, and also parents, teachers, ministers, professional counselors, scoutmasters, best friends. How do these people best love their neighbor as themselves? Readers interested in Gregory's thoughts on their relationships with God and with themselves can look at parts 1 and 2 in one of the existing translations of the entire *Regula Pastoralis*; in part 3 their relationships with others are Gregory's subject.

Perhaps I should say something about Gregory's use of Scripture. His knowledge of the Bible was both wide and deep—seldom is he at a loss for an appropriate tag to clinch an argument. This may prove a difficulty for a reader who has a sense of the integrity of biblical texts. Gregory's method should, however, be familiar to readers of the New Testament; it was the normal method of "interpretation" up

---

2. Ibid., p. 186.
3. Ibid., p. 125.

until the period of the European enlightenment. Scripture was the ultimate authority, and could be used both to prove a point and to serve as a basis for the development of an idea. Gregory uses it both ways.

I have used the Latin text established by Floribert Rommel, O.S.B., for the French series, *Sources chrétiennes*.[4] This text is based on a manuscript in the municipal library of Troyes considered to be contemporary with the author and from his milieu. It has even been suggested that certain corrections in the manuscript were made by Gregory himself. The French translation by Charles Morel, S.J., published in that volume, as well as the English translations by James Barmby[5] and Henry Davis, S.J.,[6] have been of assistance in interpreting Gregory's sometimes crabbed, and often devastatingly precise, Latin. Translations of scriptural texts are based on the New Revised Standard Version of the Bible.

I am grateful to Father Martin Boler and the monks of Mount Saviour Monastery for an extended loan of the two volumes of the *Sources chrétiennes* from their monastery library. I have worked on this translation at the Hermitage of the Dayspring in Kent, Connecticut, and at the Yale Divinity School in New Haven. To friends at both places I owe more than I can say.

John Leinenweber

---

4. *Règle pastorale,* vols. 381, 382 of *Sources chrétiennes* (Paris: Les Éditions du Cerf, 1992).

5. *The Book of Pastoral Rule,* in vol. 12 of *A Select Library of Nicene and Post-Nicene Fathers,* 2nd ser. (Grand Rapids: Eerdmans, 1978), pp. 1–72.

6. *Pastoral Care,* vol. 11 of *Ancient Christian Writers* (Westminster: Newman Press, 1950).

Prologue

I HAVE SHOWN the kind of person a pastor ought to be;[1] now let me describe how a pastor should teach. Long before my time Gregory Nazianzen, whose memory we hold in honor, taught that no single exhortation suits everyone because we are not all bound by the same character traits.[2] What helps some often harms others—plants that nourish some animals kill others; a gentle hissing that calms horses excites puppies; medicine that relieves one disease aggravates another; the bread that strengthens hardy people is fatal to the young.

Teachers have to accommodate their language to the characters of those who are listening to them so as to meet their individual needs, but they must never renounce the art of building up everyone. Listeners' minds are like the strings of a lyre. A skilled musician plucks them in a variety of ways in order to produce a song, and the reason they produce the melody is that, though they are plucked with a single plectrum, the touch is different. So too teachers ought to touch their hearers' hearts with a single teaching in order to upbuild everyone in the single virtue of love, but they should not exhort everyone in exactly the same way.

---

1. In part 2 of the *Regula Pastoralis*, not included in this volume.
2. See *Oration* 2.28–33, in *Nicene and Post-Nicene Fathers*, 2ⁿᵈ ser. vol. 7, pp. 210–11.

I

Diversity in Preaching

THE ART OF PREACHING demands great diversity.
We must counsel differently men and women; the
young and the old; the destitute and the wealthy; the
happy and the sorrowful; inferiors and superiors; servants and
masters; the worldly-wise and the simple; the presumptuous
and the diffident; the bold and the timid; the impatient and
the patient; the kind and the envious; the guileless and the
devious; the healthy and the sick; those afraid of chastisement
and who live blamelessly on that account, and those so hardened in evil that no chastisement can make them amend; the
reserved and the talkative; the indolent and the impulsive; the
meek and the irascible; the humble and the proud; the stubborn and the fickle; the gluttonous and the abstemious; those
who already give away their possessions out of compassion,
and those who even strive to seize what belongs to others;
those who neither desire others' goods nor give away their
own, and those who give away what they have while constantly seizing what belongs to others; the quarrelsome and
the peaceable; sowers of discord and peacemakers.

We must counsel differently those who wrongly interpret the words of the holy law, and those who interpret
them correctly but speak without humility; those capable of
preaching worthily but whom excessive humility holds
back, and those debarred from it by immaturity or age but
who push heedlessly on; those successful in fulfilling their

3

temporal desires, and those who, though they crave what is of the world, are worn out by toil and adversity; those bound by marriage, and those free of its ties; those who have experienced sexual intercourse, and those who have not; those who grieve over their sinful actions, and those who grieve over their sinful thoughts; those who weep for what they have done but do not stop doing it, and those who stop sinning but do not weep; those who go so far as to praise the wrong they do, and those who condemn their wrongdoing without avoiding it; those overcome by sudden desires, and those who deliberately bind themselves by their faults; those who commit small wrongs but do them frequently, and those who keep themselves from little sins while sometimes being overwhelmed by grave ones; those who do not even begin to do good, and those who do not finish what they have begun; those who secretly do wrong and publicly do good, and those who conceal the good they do, yet allow people to think ill of them as a result of certain things they do publicly.

But what good is it to run through all these in a list if I do not also, as briefly as possible, explain them one by one?

Men and Women,
Young and Old, Rich and Poor

W E MUST COUNSEL men and women differently. Men need heavy obligations and women
lighter ones; men are exercised by large undertak-
ings, while women are gently transformed by lighter ones.

We must counsel the young differently from the old.
Stern counsel often makes the young advance, while pleas-
ant entreaties move the old to do better. Scripture says, "Do
not rebuke the elderly, but entreat them as you would your
own parents."[1]

We must counsel the destitute differently from the
wealthy. We need to offer the destitute words of encouragement in the face of their affliction, while bringing the
wealthy to fear arrogance. The Lord says to the destitute
through the prophet, "Do not be afraid, you will not be
brought to nothing," and a little later he soothes them by
calling them "poor little ones, storm-tossed." Again, he is
comforting them when he tells them, "I have chosen you in
the furnace of poverty."[2]

On the other hand, Paul says to a disciple concerning the
rich, "As for those who in the present age are rich, command them not to be proud, and not to set their hopes on
the uncertainty of their riches."[3] We should note here that

---

1. 1 Tim. 5:1.
2. Isa. 54:4, 11; 48:10.
3. 1 Tim. 6:17.

the teacher of humility, when he thinks of the rich, does not tell us to "ask" but to "command" them. We owe loving-kindness to weakness, but we are not obliged to honor pride. For such people, what we can rightly say we have even more right to command, since they are buoyed up by lofty thoughts about things that pass away. The Lord says of them in the gospel, "Woe to you who are rich, for you have your consolation."[4] They take comfort in the abundance of their present life because they are unfamiliar with eternal joys.

We must offer consolation to those being purified in the furnace of poverty even as we bring fear to those lifted up on the consolations of temporal glory. The destitute need to learn that they possess riches that they do not see, while the wealthy must recognize that they have no way of retaining the riches that they do see.

Frequently, however, moral character changes the positions of the two types, and the rich become humble while the poor become proud. Preachers must quickly accommodate their words to the lives of their hearers. They should lash out more severely at the pride of the poor that not even their poverty brings down, while they foster the humility of the rich in that not even the abundance that supports them makes them proud.

Yet we must somehow appease even the proud rich with flattering exhortations. A soothing dressing will often relieve a severe wound, and a physician who humors the insane will often stop their raging; when we meet them pleasantly on their own terms, the fit of insanity is assuaged. When the evil spirit came upon Saul, David took up the lyre and relieved his raving.[5] What does Saul represent if not the pride of the powerful, and what is David if not the humble life of the saints? When Saul was seized by an unclean spirit, David's singing tempered his raving. When pride turns the disposition of the powerful to rage, we

---

4. Luke 6:24.
5. 1 Sam. 16:23; 18:10.

rightly recall them to a healthy state of mind by the calmness of our language, as if by the sweet tones of a lyre.

Sometimes when accusing the powerful of this world we have to get their attention by means of a story that appears to concern someone else. Then, when they have pronounced a judgment, as if on the other person, we must use suitable means to bring home to them their own guilt. In this way people inflated by their temporal power cannot rise up against the one who is reproving them; they have trodden on the neck of pride by their own judgment; they have no defense—their own sentence binds them.

Thus Nathan the prophet came to accuse King David, and asked his judgment, as if in the case of a poor man against a rich man.[6] He intended to have the king first deliver his sentence, and only then hear of his own guilt. Then David would not be able to contradict the judgment he had brought against himself. That holy man, Nathan, considered David both sinner and king. By his admirable plan he strove first to bind the bold culprit by an admission, and then to cut him down by an attack. He concealed for a moment the one he was after, but when he had taken him, he struck quickly.

Perhaps the blow would have had less strength if Nathan had chosen to castigate the king's fault openly from the very beginning; the intervening parable made the rebuke that he had concealed more pointed. A doctor came to a sick man, saw the wound he was to incise, but was in doubt about the patient's submissiveness. Therefore he concealed his surgeon's knife under his clothing, then suddenly drew it out and thrust it into the wound. The patient was to feel the knife piercing him before he saw it; if he had seen it first, he might have refused to feel it.

<hr />

6. 2 Sam. 12:1–7.

3

The Happy and the Sorrowful

W E MUST COUNSEL the happy and the sorrowful differently. We must show to the happy the sorrow that follows from punishment; we must show to the sorrowful the promised happiness of the kingdom. The happy must learn from our stern warnings what they have to fear; the sorrowful must hear of the joys they have to look forward to. Our Master tells the happy, "Woe to you who are laughing now, for you will weep," and the sorrowful, "I will see you again, and your hearts will rejoice, and no one will take your joy from you."[1]

Temperament, and not outward circumstances, causes some people to become happy or sorrowful. We must impress on them that certain vices accompany certain temperaments. The happy tend toward dissipation, the sorrowful toward anger. All of us, then, must consider not only the temperament we have to live with, but the worse things it exposes us to; when we fail to fight our moods we may succumb to vices from which we thought we were free.

---

1. Luke 6:25; John 16:22.

4

Inferiors and Superiors

WE MUST COUNSEL inferiors and superiors differently, the former so that their lower place does not crush them, and the latter so that they do not become proud over their superior place; inferiors, that they do not do less than they are commanded to do, superiors, that they do not command more than is just; inferiors, to submit with humility, superiors, to preside with moderation. Inferiors can take the words, "Children, obey your parents in the Lord," as directed to them, while superiors are instructed, "Parents, do not provoke your children to anger."[1] Inferiors must learn what their attitude ought to be before their hidden judge, and superiors how they are to give an example of good behavior to those committed to them.

Superiors should be aware that if ever they do wrong, they have become responsible for deaths as many as the examples of wrongdoing they have given to those in their charge. They must guard against faults with all the more care as they do not die alone from their misdeeds. We must counsel inferiors that, if they cannot be found free at least from their own faults, they will be severely punished, and superiors, that they will be judged guilty of the mistakes of those in their charge, even if they no longer find reason for concern on their own account. Since they are not involved in responsibility for others, inferiors should have more care

---

1. Eph. 6:1, 4; cf. Col. 3:20–21.

for themselves; superiors, on the other hand, are to bear their responsibility for others in such a way as to be responsible for themselves as well; they are to be fervent on their own account, while not relaxing their concern for those entrusted to them.

To those responsible only for themselves Scripture says, "Idler, go to the ant, consider its ways, and learn wisdom," while it threatens superiors with, "My child, if you have pledged yourself for your friend, you have fastened yourself to a stranger; you are snared by the words of your own mouth, caught by your own speech."[2] To pledge ourselves for a friend is to put our own life at risk by taking on another's. We fasten ourselves to a stranger when we bind ourselves to a responsibility we did not have before. We are snared by the words of our own mouths and caught by our own speech, because, when we are obliged to tell those entrusted to us what is good, we have to begin by doing everything that we say. We are snared by the words of our mouths when reason demands that our own lives be no easier than the lives of those we are counseling. In the sight of our strict judge we are bound to fulfill in our own conduct all that we enjoin on others.

And then this exhortation is immediately added: "Do then, my child, what I say, and deliver yourself, because you have fallen into your neighbor's hands. Run about, hurry, rouse your friend; give your eyes no sleep; do not let your eyelids slumber."[3] Scripture admonishes those who are set over others as examples of right living not only to watch over themselves but also to rouse their friends. Watching over themselves by living a good life is not enough; they must also free those in their charge from the lethargy of sin.

"Give your eyes no sleep; do not let your eyelids slumber." We give sleep to our eyes when we withdraw our attention and completely disregard our responsibility for

---

2. Prov. 6:6, 1–2.
3. Prov. 6:3–4.

those under us; our eyelids slumber when our thoughts are weighed down by sloth, and we connive at those things in our subordinates that we know we ought to challenge. To neither know nor correct the actions of those entrusted to us is to be fast asleep. To know what has to be censured, but not to amend it with appropriate reprimands because we find this irksome, is not to sleep but to slumber. Slumbering leads the eye into deep sleep—frequently when those set over others fail to check the evils they discern, as the just effect of their negligence they cease even to recognize the wrongdoing of those under them.

We must counsel those set over others to strive to become living creatures of heaven—those described as full of eyes round about and within[4]—by their eagerness to look all around them. For them to have eyes within and round about is fitting—as they are zealous to please their interior judge and to give a living example, they are also able to detect in others anything that needs to be corrected.

Inferiors must be counseled not to judge rashly the lives of those set over them if they should happen to observe them doing wrong. What would lead them rightly to denounce evil might by an impulse of pride plunge them into the depths. We must counsel them not to become insolent when they observe the faults of their superiors; however serious the wrongdoing, fear of God must restrain their inner judgment, and they should not refuse to bear the yoke of reverence.

I can illustrate this by bringing up the example of David.[5] When Saul, his persecutor, went into a cave to empty his bowels, David, who had so long suffered persecution from him, was inside the cave with his men. When they urged him to strike Saul down, David cut them short with the response that he ought not to lay his hand on the Lord's anointed. Even so, he rose stealthily and cut off a corner of Saul's cloak.

---

4. Rev. 4:6; Ezek. 1:18; 10:12.
5. 1 Sam. 24:1–7.

What does Saul represent if not bad counselors? David represents good subordinates. Saul's emptying of his bowels is the discharging by superiors of the evil conceived in their hearts in disgusting conduct, and the revealing of their offensive thoughts in overt actions. David feared striking Saul because loyal subordinates, who avoid in every way the plague of detraction, refrain from using their tongues as swords against those over them even as they censure their shortcomings. Sometimes, however, they lack the inner strength for this, so that they mention some extreme and obvious disorder in those over them. Even if they do this with humility, they are as it were quietly cutting off the corners of their cloaks; when they harmlessly and stealthily diminish a superior's dignity, they are as it were disfiguring the vestment of the king set over them. Then they return to themselves, and most earnestly reproach themselves for their slightest defamatory word. And so Scripture says, "Afterward David was stricken to the heart because he had cut off the corner of Saul's cloak."

We are not to strike our superiors' deeds with the sword of our mouth even when we correctly judge that they need to be censured. If we find that we have slipped, and that we have spoken against them in even the slightest way, we must humble our hearts by sorrow and repentance. In this way we return to ourselves. When we have transgressed against a superior's authority, we must dread a judgment against us by the one who submitted us to that authority. When we transgress against our superiors, we are resisting the order established by the one who set them over us. Moses, when he learned that the people were complaining against Aaron and himself, said, "What are we? Your murmuring is not against us but against the Lord."[6]

---

6. Exod. 16:8.

5

Servants and Masters

W E MUST COUNSEL servants differently from masters. Servants should be continually aware of their humble condition; masters must never lose sight of their own nature, since they and their servants have been created equal. Servants must be counseled never to spurn God by proudly opposing the order God established; masters too must be counseled that they are taking pride in God's gift, and opposing God himself, if they fail to acknowledge that those subject to them by their condition are their equals by their sharing of a common nature. We must counsel servants to be aware that they are servants of their masters; we must counsel masters to acknowledge that they are fellow servants of their servants. Scripture says, "Servants, obey your earthly masters," and again, "Let all who are under the yoke of servitude regard their masters as worthy of all honor"; it also says, "And you masters, do the same to them. Stop threatening them, for you know that both of you have the same Master in heaven."[1]

---

1. Col. 3:22; 1 Tim. 6:1; Eph. 6:9.

6

The Worldly-wise and the Simple

WE MUST COUNSEL the worldly-wise and the simple differently. The wise have to cease to know what they know, and the simple have to strive to know what they do not know. The first thing we have to destroy in the wise is their opinion that they are wise; in the simple, whatever they know of the wisdom from above has now to be upbuilt—as they are not proud, their hearts are ready, to support the building so to speak. The work of the wise is to become more wisely foolish, to abandon their foolish wisdom and to learn the wise foolishness of God; we have to preach to the simple that they must move away from what is considered foolishness, and come closer to true wisdom.

Scripture tells the wise, "If you appear to be wise in this age, you should become fools so that you may be wise," and the simple, "Not many of you are wise according to human standards," and again, "God chose what is foolish in the world to confound the wise."[1] Arguments based on reason frequently give a new direction to the wise, while example works better for the simple. The wise benefit from being brought down by their own arguments; for the simple, sometimes an awareness of the praiseworthy actions of others is enough.

Our illustrious teacher, Paul, was a debtor both to the wise and to the foolish. When counseling the Hebrews, of

---

1. 1 Cor. 3:18, 26, 27.

whom some were wise and some rather slow, he spoke to the former of the fulfillment of the Old Testament, vanquishing their wisdom by this argument: "What is obsolete and growing old is near its end." When, however, he saw that some could be attracted only by example, he added in the same letter, "The saints suffered mocking and flogging, and even chains and imprisonment. They were stoned to death, they were sawn in two, they were tempted, they were killed by the sword"; and again, "Remember your leaders, those who spoke the word of God to you; consider the outcome of their way of life, and imitate their faith."[2] Reason victorious is to break down the wise, and the attractive power of imitation is to persuade the simple to rise to greater things.

---

2. Rom. 1:14; Heb. 8:13; 11:36–37; 13:7.

7

The Presumptuous
and the Diffident

W E MUST COUNSEL the presumptuous and the diffident differently. Only a harsh rebuke is able to restrain the vice of presumption, while a modest exhortation will frequently improve the diffident. The presumptuous are only aware of their faults if they are rebuked, and even by many people; a teacher's gentle reminder of what is wrong is often enough to change the diffident. An energetic reproof does more for the presumptuous, while the diffident make better progress if we touch, as it were, obliquely on what we are reproving in them.

The Lord openly rebukes the presumptuous Jewish people: "You have the forehead of a whore; you refused to be ashamed," while he gives new strength to the diffident when he says, "You will forget the shame of your youth, and will no more remember the disgrace of your widowhood, because your Maker will possess you."[1] Paul openly rebukes the Galatians for their presumptuous transgressions: "You foolish Galatians! Who has bewitched you?"; and again, "Are you so foolish that, having started with the spirit, you are ending with the flesh?" He censures the faults of the diffident like a fellow sufferer when he says, "I rejoiced in the Lord greatly, that now at last you have revived your concern for me—as indeed you were concerned, but you were busy."[2] This was to uncover the faults of the former with a rebuke, and to veil the neglect of the latter with soft words.

---

1. Jer. 3:3; Isa. 54:4–5.
2. Gal. 3:1, 3; Phil. 4:10.

8

The Bold and the Timid

W E MUST COUNSEL the bold and the timid differently. Those who are very self-confident hold others in disdain and reproach them; those who are too much aware of their own weakness frequently fall into despondency. The bold consider that everything they do is of the highest excellence; the timid regard what they are doing as extremely contemptible, and despondency crushes them.

We must offer an astute criticism of the actions of the bold to show that their self-satisfaction is displeasing to God. We correct them best when we show that in fact they did badly what they believe they did well; in this way what they believe deserved praise may lead to a helpful confusion. Sometimes, when they are completely unaware of having this vice, they more quickly amend if they are shamed by being charged with another, more obvious fault; then, as they are unable to defend this fault, they may recognize that they are wrong to uphold the one they are defending.

Paul, seeing that the Corinthians were overbold and puffed up against one another—some were claiming to belong to Apollos, some to Paul, some to Cephas, and some to Christ—brought up the sin of incest that had been committed in their midst, and that remained uncorrected. He says, "A case of sexual immorality is reported among you of a kind not found even among pagans—one of you is living with his father's wife. And you are puffed up, and not rather in mourning, that the one who has done this may be removed from among you."[1] He is asking them, "Why, through your boldness, do you say that you belong to this one or that one when, by your irresolution and negligence, you demonstrate that you belong to none of them?"

On the other hand, we are more apt to bring the timid to right ways of acting if we search indirectly for some of their good points. Then, as we correct some things in them by our reproofs, we warmly praise others. In this way the praise they hear fosters their sensitive feelings, which the fault we have rebuked is chastening. Usually we make better progress with these people if we recall their good deeds, and, if they have done something out of order, we do not reprimand them as if for a fault they have already committed, but we prohibit it as something they are not to do in the future. Thus our appreciation will encourage what we approve of, and a modest exhortation will count more with them against what we censure.

When Paul learned that the Thessalonians were remaining true to the preaching they had received, but were shaken by a kind of timidity, as if by reason of the nearness of the end of the world, he first praised what he saw was strong in them, and afterward fortified what was weak by his discreet counsel. He said, "We must always give thanks to God for you, brothers and sisters, as is right, because your faith is growing abundantly, and the love of every one of you for one another is increasing. Therefore we ourselves boast of your patience and faith among the churches of God." After setting down these flattering remarks concerning their lives, he added, "We beg you, brothers and sisters, by the coming of our Lord Jesus Christ, and of our being gathered together in him, not to be easily shaken in mind or alarmed, either by spirits, or by word, or by letter, as though from us, to the effect that the day of the Lord is already here."[2]

---

1. 1 Cor. 1:12; 5:1–2.
2. 2 Thess. 1:3–4; 2:1–2.

Paul was acting like a true teacher. First they heard themselves praised for something they were able to call to mind, and afterward they were exhorted to go in a certain direction. The praise given first was to settle them so that they would not be shaken by the admonition that was to follow. Paul knew that they were disturbed by their suspicion of the end being near, but he did not blame them for it. Instead, as if he was ignorant of their state, he forbade them to be disturbed in the future. They believed that their preacher was unaware of their groundless anxiety, while he wanted them to be as much afraid of incurring blame as they were of his coming to know of it.

9

The Impatient and the Patient

W E MUST CORRECT the impatient and the patient differently. We must tell the impatient that when they neglect to restrain themselves they are dragged through whole abysses of injustice, even without intending it, because their rage drives them places they have no desire to go. As if unaware of what they are doing, people in their disturbed state do what afterward, when their awareness has returned, they regret.

We must also tell them that when they are driven on by their emotions they act as if they are strangers to themselves, and afterward they hardly recognize the evils they have done. When they fail to oppose their passions they distort the good they accomplished when they were calm; by obeying their heedless impulses they tear down what they may, perhaps with long and prudent toil, have built up.

The virtue of love, the mother and guardian of all virtues, is lost through the vice of impatience. Scripture tells us that "love is patient," and so love does not exist where patience is absent. Learning, the nurse of the virtues, is squandered by this vice of impatience. Scripture says that "a person's learning is known by patience."[1] People prove by their lack of patience that they lack learning. No one who cannot bear others' evils tranquilly can truly impart good by teaching.

---

1. 1 Cor. 13:4; Prov. 19:11 Vulgate.

Arrogance frequently pierces a person through this vice of impatience. People who do not permit themselves to be disregarded in this world try to reveal their good points, if they have any that are hidden, and are thus led by impatience to arrogance. As they are unable to bear being overlooked, they ostentatiously boast in self-display. On this point Scripture says that "the patient are better than the proud."[2] The patient have chosen to suffer any evil rather than have their hidden good points become known through the vice of ostentation. By contrast, the arrogant choose to have good spoken of them, even falsely, rather than suffer the slightest evil.

When people relinquish patience, even the good they have done up to that time is destroyed. That is why Ezekiel was shown that there was to be a hollow space in the altar where the holocaust laid on it might be kept safe.[3] In the absence of the hollow, a passing breeze might disperse any sacrifice found there. What do we take God's altar to be if not the souls of the just? They lay upon themselves a sacrifice in God's sight as often as they do a good deed. What is the hollow in the altar if not the patience of the good? When they humble themselves in order to endure hardships they show that they are in a very low place, as if in the bottom of a ditch. The altar must contain a hollow, then, so that the air will not disperse the sacrifice laid upon it. That means that the elect must remain patient so that they will not be disturbed by the wind of impatience and lose all the good that they have done.

We are told that this is a hollow of a single cubit, and if we do not forsake patience we preserve the measure of unity. Paul says, "Bear one another's burdens, and in this way you will fulfill the law of Christ." The law of Christ is the love that is unity; only those who do not transgress even when oppressed fulfill it. Let the impatient listen to

---

2. Eccl. 7:8.
3. Ezek. 43:13 Vulgate.

Scripture: "The patient are better than the valiant, and those who are masters of themselves are better than those who capture cities."[4] A victory over cities is of less value because what is subjected is external; far greater is what is conquered by patience, because when patience compels us to govern ourselves, we overcome ourselves, and become subject to ourselves.

Let the impatient listen to what Truth told his chosen disciples: "By your patience will you possess your souls."[5] We have been so wonderfully fashioned that reason possesses the soul, and the soul possesses the body. The soul, however, is dispossessed of its right over the body if it is not first possessed by reason. The Lord showed us that patience is the guardian of our state when he taught us to possess ourselves in patience. We can see, then, the magnitude of the fault of impatience, since by our impatience we lose possession of what we are.

The impatient should listen to these further words of Solomon: "A fool gives full vent to his mind, but the wise wait and hold back for later."[6] Under the influence of impatience people vent their whole mind outwardly; because they lack the inner discipline of wisdom to hold them in, their emotions quickly erupt. "The wise wait and hold back for later." When they have received an injury they do not want immediate revenge because, since they are tolerant, they choose to bear up and have mercy; still, they are aware that everything will be fairly brought to rights at the final judgment.

On the other hand, we must counsel the patient not to complain internally over what they are putting up with externally. They are offering outwardly a perfect sacrifice of great value, and must not spoil it inwardly by the disease of malice. People may not notice, but God judges this a sin.

---

4. Gal. 6:2–3; Prov. 16:32.
5. Luke 21:19.
6. Prov. 29:11.

Complaining is a fault that becomes worse the more people parade their virtues before others.

We must then tell the patient that they are to strive to love those they must of necessity bear with. If love fails to accompany patience, the virtue we are exhibiting may turn into the more harmful fault of hatred. When Paul says that "love is patient" he immediately adds "and kind." He is pointing out that we must not cease to love out of our kindness those we bear with out of our patience. This great teacher, when urging patience on his disciples, says, "Put away from you all bitterness and wrath and anger and wrangling and slander"; then, as if all external matters are now in order, he turns inward and adds, "together with all malice."[7] We waste our time putting away anger, wangling, and slander outwardly if malice, the mother of vices, continues to rule us inwardly. Cutting wickedness away from the branches outside is useless if it remains inside in the root, ready to rise up in more various ways.

And so Truth tells us in his own words, "Love your enemies, do good to those who hate you, pray for those who persecute and abuse you."[8] To put up with our adversaries is a virtue before humans; to love them is a virtue before God. God accepts only the sacrifice that he sees enkindled on the altar of good works by the flame of love. That is why he asks some people who are patient but not loving, "Why do you see the speck in your neighbor's eye, and not the log in your own eye?" Impatience is the speck, malice in the heart is the log. The breeze of temptation stirs the speck; confirmed wickedness makes the log almost impossible to remove. Therefore he was right to add, "You hypocrite, first take the log out of your own eye, and then you will see clearly to take the speck out of your neighbor's eye."[9] He is saying to the wicked who complain inwardly as they display

---

7. 1 Cor. 13:4; Eph. 4:31.
8. Luke 6:27–28; Matt. 5:44.
9. Matt. 7:3, 5; Luke 6:41–42.

themselves as saints by their outward patience, "First shake off your heavy weight of malice, and then blame others for their light fault of impatience. If you do not strive to overcome your hypocrisy, putting up with the wrongdoing of others will be worse for you."

For the patient to be untroubled at the moment they experience some opposition or hear some insult is not unusual—they are giving evidence of their patience while preserving the integrity of their hearts. Later, however, when they recall what they have endured, they are inflamed with resentment and seek reasons for taking revenge. They retract the meekness with which they suffered, and turn it into malice.

Preachers can aid these people more quickly if they explain the cause of this change. Our cunning adversary brings about a war against two persons, rousing one to inflict an injury, then provoking the one who has been injured to return it. Frequently, however, while he is already victor over the one he has persuaded to inflict the injury, he is conquered by the one who bears with equanimity what has been inflicted. Therefore our adversary, conqueror of the one he has subjugated by his provocation, is irritated by the firm and triumphant resistance offered by the other, and rises up with all his might. Since he was unable to stir up the injured person when the injury occurred, he rests for a time from the open contest; relying on secret suggestions to disturb this one's mind, he seeks a suitable time for his deception. Because he has lost in the public war, he is on fire to lay hidden snares. During a period of tranquillity he returns to the victor's mind and recalls the loss of possessions or the injuries, greatly exaggerating the whole thing, and showing that it was intolerable. He so vexes his victim's mind that often the patient one, taken captive after being a victor, is ashamed at having borne everything with equanimity, and regrets not having returned the injuries. If an opportunity should occur, the injured person would seek to do even worse.

To whom can we liken these people if not to those whose bravery makes them victors on the field of battle, but who afterward are captured, through their carelessness, within the confines of the city? Whom do they resemble if not those attacked by a serious illness, who survive it only to die of a recurrence of the fever as it comes gently on?

We must then counsel the patient to fortify their hearts after a victory, and to keep an eye on the enemy. They have overcome him in public warfare, but he is preparing an ambush against their inner defenses. They must fear having their illness creep back upon them. Then our cunning enemy will rejoice with more joy in his later deception, in that he is treading on the necks of his conquerors, which had long been raised up against him.

The Kind and the Envious

W E MUST COUNSEL the kind and the envious differently. We must counsel the kind so to rejoice with others in the good they have in them that they long to make it their own. They must praise their neighbors' deeds by love and multiply them by imitation. If they are present at the race[1]—that is, at this life—as fervent partisans of others, but inactive spectators, they will remain unrewarded after the contest since they did not exert themselves in it. Then they will be troubled to see the palms of victory awarded to those now exerting themselves even as they remain idle. We commit a grave sin if we do not appreciate the good actions of others; we have no reward at all if we do not imitate, to the best of our ability, what we appreciate.

We must tell the kind that if they are not quick to imitate the good that they applaud, their pleasure in the holiness of the virtuous is just like the pleasure that foolish spectators find in the vain skill of public performers. These people shower charioteers and actors with favors without, however, having the least desire to be like them. They admire those who do something they enjoy, but are not willing to provide the same kind of enjoyment to others. We must tell the kind that when they see what their neighbors do they must return to their own hearts and not count on those others; they should not praise what is good while

---

1. 1 Cor. 9:24.

refusing to do it. At the end, the punishment of those unwilling to imitate what has brought them delight will be very severe.

We must counsel the envious to weigh carefully the blindness of those disheartened by the progress of others, those who pine away when others rejoice. How wretched are those who grow worse as their neighbors improve! They are afflicted by anxiety as they observe the growing success of others, and they die of a disease of their own hearts. What is more unhappy than those disturbed by the sight of happiness and whose torment makes them worse?

If they loved others, the good that belongs to those others would become their own. Just as many parts make up one body,[2] so do all human beings live in the faith; their functions are various, but by being adapted to one another they become one. As a result, the foot sees by means of the eyes, and the eyes get about by means of the feet. The hearing of the ears serves the mouth, and the tongue works together with the ears for their benefit. The stomach sustains the hands, and the hands work for the stomach. From the very composition of our body we learn what we are meant to observe in our conduct. We ought, then, to be extremely ashamed not to resemble what we are. What we value in others—even what we are unable to copy—belongs to us; whatever people value in us becomes the possession of those who value it. The envious must measure the power of love—it makes the result of others' toil our own without our having to toil for it!

We must tell the envious that when they do not keep themselves from jealousy they are sunk in the ancient wickedness of our wily enemy. Scripture says of him, "Through the devil's envy death entered the world."[3] Because he lost heaven, he begrudges it to created human beings; being ruined himself, he adds to his damnation by ruining others.

---

2. 1 Cor. 12:14–27.
3. Wisd. of Sol. 2:24.

We must counsel the envious so that they may know how many pitfalls and what gradually increasing ruin they are liable to because, as they do not cast envy from their hearts, they are sinking down to actions that are clearly wicked. If Cain had not envied his brother's acceptable offering he would not have reached the point of taking away his life. Scripture says, "And the Lord had regard for Abel and his offering, but for Cain and his offering he had no regard. So Cain was exceedingly angry, and his countenance fell."[4] Envy of a sacrifice caused a fratricide. Cain was sorry that his brother was better than himself, and he cut him off from life.

We must tell the envious that while they are inwardly consumed by that plague they are also destroying whatever good they may appear to have in themselves. Scripture says, "A sound heart gives life to the flesh, but envy makes the bones rot."[5] What does flesh represent if not weak and delicate action, and what do bones represent if not stalwart action? Frequently people with innocent hearts appear weak in some of their actions, while those who display stouteheartedness to human eyes are inwardly consumed by the pestilence of envy of the success of others. "A sound heart gives life to the flesh," because if we preserve our innocence, even what is outwardly weak may some day be strengthened. "Envy makes the bones rot," because through the vice of envy even what appears strong to human eyes perishes in God's sight. That bones rot through envy means that even what is strong comes to nothing.

---

4. Gen. 4:4–5.
5. Prov. 14:30.

11

The Guileless and the Devious

W E MUST COUNSEL the guileless and the devi- ous differently. We have to praise the guileless because they are eager never to tell a falsehood, but we need to counsel them sometimes to withhold the truth. As falsity invariably injures those who speak it, so truth sometimes harms those who hear it. For this reason the Lord tempered his speech with silence in the presence of his disciples: "I have many things to say to you, but you cannot bear them now."[1]

We must therefore counsel the guileless that, as avoiding deceit is always profitable, so should they always make the truth known profitably. Our counsel must be to add practical wisdom to the blessing of simplicity—then they will possess the security that comes from simplicity without losing the common sense that belongs to prudence. The teacher of the Gentiles says, "I want you to be wise in what is good, and guileless in what is evil," and Truth himself counsels his chosen ones, "Be wise as serpents and simple as doves."[2] The serpent's shrewdness must sharpen the dove's simplicity in the hearts of the chosen, and the dove's simplicity must moderate the serpent's shrewdness. In this way prudence will not seduce them into cunning, nor will simplicity dull their lively minds.

---

1. John 16:12.
2. Rom. 16:19; Matt. 10:16.

On the other hand, we must so counsel the devious that they may recognize that the duplicity they guiltily carry is hard work. As they are afraid of being found out, they are always looking for dishonest defenses and troubled by fearful suspicions. No defense is more reliable than innocence, and nothing is easier to speak than truth. When people are forced to defend their deceit their hearts are wearied with hard labor. In this context Scripture says, "The labor of their lips will overwhelm them." What satisfies them now later overwhelms them; what provides them now with a mild disquiet later oppresses them with a bitter recompense. So Jeremiah says, "They have taught their tongues to speak lies, they have labored to do wrong."[3] He means that those who could be friends of truth without labor, labor to sin; when they refuse to live without guile, their labor brings about their deaths. Ordinarily when they are taken in some fault they avoid being recognized for what they are, and they conceal themselves under a veil of deceit; they attempt to excuse their sin, even though it is perfectly obvious. Those who aim to correct their faults, which have been concealed by mists of falsity, will often find themselves losing almost all certainty concerning them.

As if he were speaking to Judah, the prophet spoke out against those sinning and excusing themselves when he said, "There the hedgehog has its hole."[4] The hedgehog represents the duplicity of the devious, who cunningly defend themselves. When you catch a hedgehog you see its head, its feet, and its whole body, but as soon as you grab it it rolls up into a ball, draws in its feet and hides its head; its entire being, all of which you saw a moment before, is lost in the hand of the person holding it.

Such indeed, such are the devious when they are caught in their transgressions. You see the hedgehog's head because you see from what starting point the sinners move toward

---

3. Ps. 140:9; Jer. 9:5.
4. Isa. 34:15 Vulgate.

their fault; its feet are conspicuous, because you recognize the steps by which they carry out their wicked deeds—and yet by the excuses the devious immediately bring forward, they draw them in, concealing all traces of their iniquity.

The hedgehog draws in its head when the devious give evidence by their wondrous defenses that they have not initiated any wickedness. It remains like a ball in the hand of the one holding it when those who are disciplining them suddenly lose everything they have learned and hold the sinner rolled up within their own consciousness; those who saw the whole at the moment they seized it are now ignorant of everything, duped by shifty and wicked pleas. The hedgehog has its hole among the worthless because the duplicity of a malicious mind rolls up and hides in the darkness of its defenses.

Let the devious listen to the words of Scripture: "Whoever walks in integrity walks securely." Acting with integrity assures us of great security. Let them hear the words of one of the wise: "The holy spirit of discipline will flee from deceit." Let them hear the affirmation of Scripture: "The Lord converses with the guileless."[5] For God, to converse is to reveal his secrets to human minds by the light of his presence. He is said to converse with the guileless because the ray of his visitation enlightens the minds of people dimmed by no shadow of duplicity with knowledge of the mysteries of heaven. The particular evil of the duplicitous is that, while they are deceiving others by their false and deceitful actions, they pride themselves on having more common sense than all those around them. Because they are unaware of the severe retribution awaiting them these wretched folk rejoice in their own loss.

Let them hear how the prophet Zephaniah threatens them with the power of divine chastisement: "See, the great and terrible day of the Lord is coming; that day of wrath, a day of darkness and gloom, a day of cloud and whirlwind,

---

5. Prov. 10:9; Wisd. of Sol. 1:5; Prov. 3:32.

a day of trumpet blast and battle cry against all the fortified cities and against all the lofty corner towers."[6] What does he mean by the fortified cities if not suspicious minds that are always surrounded by a deceitful defense? As often as one of their faults is attacked they deflect the missile of truth. And what do the corner towers represent—a corner being always made up of two walls—if not devious hearts? When these flee the simplicity of truth they fold back on themselves with a kind of perverse duplicity, and, what is worse, out of the very fault of deviousness they pride themselves on their scornful prudence!

And so the day of the Lord, a day full of vengeance and chastisement, is coming against the fortified cities and against the lofty corner towers. The wrath of the final judgment will destroy those human hearts whose defenses have closed them against the truth, and it will demolish those enveloped in duplicity. Then will the fortified cities collapse, because those whom God has not penetrated will be condemned. Then will lofty corner towers fall to the ground, because the sentence of justice will throw down hearts that raise themselves up by their false prudence.

---

6. Zeph. 1:14–16.

12

The Healthy and the Sick

WE MUST COUNSEL the healthy and the sick differently. We must counsel the healthy to use their sound bodies for the sake of having sound souls. If they should turn the gift of their good health to an evil end, they would become worse by virtue of the gift. Because of it they would later deserve a heavier punishment in that they are not now afraid to make a bad use of so generous a gift from God.

We must counsel the healthy not to take lightly their chance to earn eternal salvation. Scripture says, "See, now is the acceptable time; see, now is the day of salvation!" We must counsel them that if they are unwilling to please God when they can, later on when they wish to do so they may not be able. Wisdom abandons those who have too long refused her call: "I called, and you refused; I stretched out my hand, and no one took notice. You disdained all my counsel and neglected my rebukes; I also will laugh at your ruin, and I will mock when what you feared comes upon you." Again, "Then they will call upon me, but I will not hear; they will rise early, and they will not find me."[1] If we disregard the bodily health given us for doing good, we will realize the value of the gift when we have lost it; when at the opportune time we have held it unprofitably, at the end we will look for it in vain.

---

1. 2 Cor. 6:2; Prov. 1:24–26, 28.

Again, Solomon says, "Do not give your honor to strangers and your years to one who is cruel; otherwise strangers may be filled with your strength, and your labors be in an alien house; and you will groan in the last days, when you have consumed your flesh and your body."[2] Who are strangers to us if not the evil spirits who have been excluded from our heavenly country? What is our honor if not that, even as we have been made in bodies of clay, we have been created in the image and likeness of our maker? Who else is cruel but the apostate angel, who by his pride struck himself with the pain of death, and, even after he was lost, did not forbear bringing death on the human race? Those people give their honor to strangers who, even though they have been created in the image and likeness of God, order the circumstances of their lives according to the pleasure of evil spirits. They also deliver their years to one who is cruel when they spend the span of life they have received at the good pleasure of an adversary who dominates them for wrong.

The text rightly says that "otherwise strangers may be filled with your strength, and your labors be in an alien house." Those who employ the physical well-being and wisdom they have been given in perpetrating vices, not in practicing virtues, add by their strength to the habitations of strangers and not to their own houses—that is to say, they multiply the deeds of unclean spirits by acting out of licentiousness or of pride, increasing the number of those who are lost by the addition of themselves.

And it adds, "and you will groan in the last days, when you have consumed your flesh and your body." Very often people expend their physical well-being on their vices; suddenly their health is gone, their flesh is weighed down by afflictions, the soul is impelled to depart—then they seek their lost health, which they possessed badly for so long, for the purpose of living well. Then—at the moment they are

---

2. Prov. 5:9–11.

unable to recover by service what they have lost by negligence—people groan because they have been unwilling to serve God. So Scripture says in another place, "When God slew them, then they sought him."[3]

On the other hand, we must counsel the sick that even as they are being chastened by the scourge of discipline they should realize that they are God's children. If God was not disposed to give an inheritance to those who have been reformed he would not be concerned to educate them by their afflictions. So the Lord tells John through the angel, "I reprimand and discipline those whom I love." So, again, Scripture says, "My child, do not make light of the Lord's discipline, or lose heart when you are reproved by him, for the Lord chastises those whom he loves, and he scourges every child whom he accepts." The psalmist tells us, "Many are the afflictions of the righteous," and blessed Job cries out in his pain, "If I am righteous I will not lift up my head, filled as I am with affliction and misery."[4]

We must tell the sick that if they believe that the heavenly country is theirs they have to experience suffering here as in an alien land. The stones for the Lord's temple were dressed outside so that they could be set in place during construction without the sound of a hammer.[5] We are now being dressed outside by ordeals so that afterward, within the Lord's temple, we may be set in place without the blows of discipline. These blows must now remove whatever is excessive in us, and then the concord of love alone will hold us fast in the building.

We must counsel the sick to consider the hard discipline we apply to our children after the flesh for the sake of an earthly inheritance. What hardship coming from divine discipline will we find grievous, then, when it both brings us an inheritance we are never to lose, and takes from us a

---

3. Ps. 78:34.
4. Rev. 3:19; Heb. 12:5–6; Ps. 34:19; Job 10:15.
5. 1 Kings 6:7.

punishment that will always endure? Paul says, "We had human parents to instruct us, and we respected them; should we not much more submit to the Father of spirits and live? They indeed instructed us for a period of a few days according to their own pleasure, but he does it for our good, that we may receive his sanctification."[6]

We must counsel the sick to consider how much well-being of heart lies in the body's affliction. Affliction calls us back to knowledge of ourselves, and revives the memory of infirmity that well-being commonly dispels. When we are drawn outside ourselves in pride, the ordeals we endure in the flesh remind us of the conditions to which we are subject.

This was shown to Balaam—if only he had been willing to follow God's voice by obeying!—when his journey was delayed. Balaam was on his way to fulfill his purpose, but the animal he sat on defeated his intention. The ass, stopped by a prohibition, saw an angel the human failed to see.[7] The flesh, dulled by its afflictions, often indicates to the mind by its ordeal a God whom the mind itself, which directs the flesh, fails to see. Thus the flesh impedes the anxious concerns of those who want to advance in this world as though proceeding on a journey until they recognize the invisible being that stands in their way.

Scripture rightly says, in Peter's words, that Balaam "had a dumb beast of burden as a rebuke to his madness; speaking with a human voice it forbade the prophet's folly."[8] A dumb beast of burden rebukes madness when their afflicted flesh reminds the proud of the value of humility, which they have to retain. Balaam did not obtain the benefit of this rebuke because, as he proceeded on his way to curse Israel, he changed his words but not his spirit.

We must counsel the sick to consider how great a gift physical affliction is—it does away with sins committed,

---

6. Heb. 12:9–10.
7. Num. 22:23.
8. 2 Pet. 2:16.

and suppresses those that could be committed. It inflicts wounds of repentance on a spirit struck by blows received from outside. Scripture says, "The livid marks of a wound cleanse away evil, as do blows in the inmost parts of the belly."[9] The livid marks of a wound cleanse away evil because the pain caused by scourges does away with wickedness, whether this is under consideration or has actually been carried out. We are used to calling the mind a belly because, just as the belly consumes food, so does the mind digest our concerns by working them over.

This verse of Scripture teaches us to call the mind a belly: "The human spirit is the lamp of the Lord, which searches all the hidden things of the belly."[10] This means that the enlightenment of divine inspiration, when it comes to a human mind, reveals the mind to itself as it enlightens; before the coming of the Holy Spirit this mind could bear vicious thoughts without knowing how to weigh them. "The livid marks of a wound cleanse away evil, as do blows in the inmost parts of the belly," because, when we are struck on the outside we—silent and afflicted—are reminded of our sins, and we bring before our eyes again all the wrongs we have done. What we suffer outwardly produces more inward grief over what we have done. Hence, along with the obvious wounds of the body, a secret blow in the belly purifies us more fully because the hidden wound of grief heals our wickedness and our vicious actions.

We must counsel the sick that in order to preserve the virtue of patience they must continually ponder the great evils our Redeemer endured from those whom he had created. How many vile insults and reproaches did he sustain! How many blows he received from those who were taunting him, while he was daily seizing captives out of the hand of the ancient enemy! While washing us with the water of salvation he did not hide his face from the spittle of the

---

9. Prov. 20:30.
10. Prov. 20:27.

faithless; while freeing us from eternal torments by his defense of us he silently endured scourging; while giving us everlasting honor among the choirs of angels he put up with buffeting; while saving us from being pierced by our sins he did not refuse to submit his head to thorns; while making us drunk with eternal sweetness he accepted the bitterness of gall in his thirst; while for our sake he was adoring the Father, even though in his divine nature he was the Father's equal, he was silent when people mockingly adored him; while preparing life for the dead, he, life itself, went to his death.

Why do we believe it hard to endure chastisement from God for our wicked deeds if God bore such great evils from us for his good deeds? What person of sound understanding is ungrateful when struck if the one who lived here without sin did not depart from here without a scourging?

13

Chastisement

WE MUST COUNSEL DIFFERENTLY those afraid of chastisement and who live blamelessly on that account, and those so hardened in evil that no chastisement can make them amend. We must say to those who fear chastisement that they should not desire temporal goods, as if these are of great value, when they see that even the wicked possess them, nor should they flee as intolerable the present evils that they know perfectly well often touch even the good here on earth.

We must counsel them that if they truly desire to escape evil they must dread eternal torments. They are not to rest in this fear of torments, however, but be nursed by charity to grow into the grace of love. Scripture says that "perfect love casts out fear," and again, "You did not receive a spirit of slavery to fall back into fear, but you received a spirit of adoption as children, by which we cry, Abba! Father!" The same teacher tells us that "where the Spirit of the Lord is, there is freedom."[1]

If fear of punishment goes on preventing evil actions, clearly those who are fearful have no liberty of spirit. Without the fear of punishment they would surely commit the fault. Those enslaved by fear do not know the grace of liberty. We are to love the good for its own sake, not pursue it under pressure of punishment. Those who do good

---

1. 1 John 4:18; Rom. 8:15; 2 Cor. 3:17.

because they are afraid of the evils of torture would prefer to have what they are afraid of cease to exist—then they could boldly do what is forbidden. That these people lose their integrity before God is clearer than day, since in his sight their desire is sin.

On the other hand, we must address more pointed words to those unrestrained even by chastisement since they are more hardened by moral insensitivity. Ordinarily we must show them scorn without scorning them, and despair of them without despairing. Then the despair we show may at least inspire them with fear, and the counsel we add may restore their hope. We must bring against them the severe judgments of God so that they may be recalled to a knowledge of themselves by thoughts of eternal punishment. They must hear that the Scripture, "If you crush a fool in a mortar, as a pestle grinds barley, the folly will not be driven out," is fulfilled in them. The prophet complains of these people to the Lord, saying, "You wore them down, and they refused to take correction." This is what the Lord says: "I have slain and destroyed that people, and yet they have not turned back from their ways," and again, "The people did not turn back to the one who struck them."[2]

The prophet complains in the voice of those who confer chastisement, "We looked after Babylon, but it was not healed." Babylon is looked after but not restored to health when those thrown into confusion by their evildoing hear words of reproach and feel the stings of reproof, and yet scorn to return to the straight road of salvation. The Lord upbraids the people of Israel who were captive yet did not turn away from their iniquity: "The house of Israel has been turned to dross for me; all of them, bronze, tin, iron, and lead, in the middle of the furnace."[3]

Put more clearly, he is saying, "I wanted to purify them in the fire of adversity, and I looked for them to become

---

2. Prov. 27:22; Jer. 5:3; 15:7; Isa. 9:13.
3. Jer. 51:9; Ezek. 22:18.

silver and gold, but they have been turned into bronze, tin, iron, and lead for me while in the furnace. Even in adversity they have come out vice, not virtue."

Bronze, when struck, returns more sound than other metals; those people, then, who break out in the sound of complaints when struck are turned to bronze in the middle of the furnace. Tin, worked with art, gives a false impression of silver; those whom adversity does not free from the vice of pretense become tin in the furnace. Iron is used by those who plot against their neighbor's life; not to lose in adversity the evil intention of doing harm is to be iron in the furnace. Lead is heavier than other metals; those who are so oppressed by the weight of their sins that even in adversity they cannot rise above earthly desires are found to be lead in the furnace.

So again, Scripture says, "Much sweat has been expended, and the thick rust has not left it, not even by fire." The Lord brings upon us the fire of adversity to cleanse us of the rust of our vices. We do not lose the rust even by fire when, in the midst of chastisement, we are not freed from vice. So the prophet says, "In vain does the refiner refine; their malice is not purged out."[4]

We should be aware, however, that sometimes people who make no improvement even when being harshly chastised are softened by a gentle word of caution. Mildness and charm will sometimes restrain from evil those whom suffering does not correct. Lukewarm water will often restore to their original good health the sick whom a strong dose of some drug has been unable to cure, and some wounds that an incision cannot cure are healed by applications of oil. Also, the hard diamond cannot be cut by metal, but it is softened by the mild blood of goats.[5]

---

4. Ezek. 24:12; Jer. 6:29.
5. Augustine *City of God* 21.4; Pliny *Natural History* 37. 59.

14

The Reserved and the Talkative

W E MUST COUNSEL the reserved and the talkative differently. The reserved have to be made to realize that while they are heedlessly avoiding some vices they are unwittingly involving themselves in worse ones. In general, when they restrain their tongues overmuch they tolerate a more dangerous talkativeness in their hearts, and their thoughts seethe in proportion to the violence by which they injudiciously hold them in. They often allow their thoughts more latitude because they think that no outside critic can observe them. Sometimes this leads them to become proud and to despise as weaklings those they hear speaking up. They fail to perceive how pride opens them up to vices even as they shut their mouths. They hold their tongues and swell their minds; they pay no attention to their own bad qualities, but in their hearts they arraign everyone else more freely as they are doing it in secret.

And so we must counsel the reserved to try to be aware not only of how they appear outwardly but also of how they ought to reveal themselves inwardly. Then they will be more afraid of a secret judgment of their own thoughts than of the criticism given their words by those around them. Scripture says, "My child, be attentive to my wisdom, and incline your ear to my understanding, so that you may guard your thoughts." Nothing in us is more truant that the heart—it deserts us every time it slips into bad thoughts.

The psalmist says, "My heart has failed me," and as he returns to himself he says, "Your servant has found his heart to pray to you."[1] When we confine our thoughts under careful guard we find our habitually truant hearts.

When the reserved suffer some injustice they often experience greater pain because they do not talk about what they are enduring. If they were to speak calmly of their troubles their pain would fade from their consciousness. Closed wounds cause more suffering—when we expel an infection burning inside the pain is made accessible to healing. Those more reserved than is good for them should realize this, and then they will not increase their pain by holding their tongues while they are enduring troubles.

We must counsel that if people love their neighbors as themselves they must not keep from them the reasons they rightly find fault with them. The medicine of their words then promotes the health of both—on the one side, bad conduct is stopped, and on the other, the opening of the wound relieves the intensity of the pain. Those who perceive evil in their neighbors and yet impose silence on themselves are like people who withhold medicines from wounds they see. Because they have chosen not to cure an infection they could cure, they become causes of death.

We must restrain our tongues judiciously, not tie them up so that they cannot be loosed. Scripture says, "The wise remain silent until the right moment"—that is, when they judge it opportune they set aside the discipline of silence and make themselves helpful by speaking suitable words. Again Scripture says, "There is a time to speak and a time to keep silence." We have to weigh the moment, so that we neither pour out our words unhelpfully when we ought to restrain ourselves, nor slothfully restrain ourselves when we could say something helpful. Taking account of this the psalmist says, "Set a guard over my mouth, O Lord, and a

---

1. Prov. 5:1; Ps. 40:12; 2 Sam. 7:27.

door of discretion to my lips."[2] He asks to have a door, something that opens and closes, set over his mouth, not a wall. We must then take care to learn how at appropriate times words should open our mouths, and how at other times esteem for silence should close them.

On the other hand, we must counsel those who spend their time in talking to observe carefully their moral decline as they spill out a host of words. The human spirit is like water—when confined it rises, seeking the level from which it fell, but when released it disperses, spreading out uselessly over the lowest levels. Unnecessary words that dissipate the discipline of silence are like so many rivulets carrying the human spirit outside itself.

For this reason the talkative are incapable of turning inward toward self-knowledge. Those who disperse themselves in talk are excluded from the secret place of inner reflection. Because they are unprotected by any wall, they are totally open to the blows of the enemy who lies in wait for them. So Scripture says, "Like a city lying open, without walls, are those unable to restrain themselves when they speak."[3] Since it lacks a wall of silence, the spiritual city lies open to the enemy's missiles, and when by its words it casts itself outside, it reveals its openness to the adversary. The enemy then overcomes that city with less effort, since by its talkativeness the city being conquered is fighting against itself.

Since the lazy ordinarily lapse by degrees, when we neglect to guard against idle words we come to harmful ones. First we take pleasure in talking about the affairs of others; later we make mordant and disparaging remarks concerning the lives of the people we talk about; and lastly we bring forth obvious slanders. By this we sow disagreements, bring about quarrels, enkindle hatreds, and extinguish peace in people's hearts. Solomon is right to say that "one who

---

2. Sirach 20:7; Eccl. 3:7; Ps. 141:3.
3. Prov. 25:28.

lets out waters is a source of strife." To let out water is to loosen one's tongue in a flood of words. In the opposite sense Solomon says, "The words of a man's mouth are deep waters." "One who lets out waters is a source of strife" because those who do not restrain their tongues put concord to flight. In opposition to this Scripture says, "One who silences a fool assuages enmities."[4]

The prophet testifies that those given to talkativeness are utterly unable to keep to the straight path of righteousness: "The talkative have no direction on earth." Again, Solomon says that "when words are many, sin is not lacking," and Isaiah, that "the practice of righteousness is silence," giving us to understand that we forsake righteousness of spirit when we do not abstain from immoderate speaking. Hence James says, "If any think that they are religious, and do not bridle their tongues but deceive their hearts, their religion is worthless." Again, he says, "Let everyone be quick to listen and slow to speak." And again, describing the power of the tongue, he adds that it is "a restless evil, full of deadly poison." Truth counsels us in his own name when he says, "On the day of judgment people will have to give an account for every idle word they utter."[5] An idle word is one not justified by any real need or intended for any holy service. If an accounting will be required for our idle words, we must consider the punishment reserved for talkativeness, in which we sin by our harmful words as well.

---

4. Prov. 17:14; 18:4; 26:10.
5. Ps. 140:11; Prov. 10:19; Isa. 32:17; James 1:26, 19; 3:8; Matt. 12:36.

15

The Indolent and the Impulsive

W E MUST COUNSEL the indolent and the impulsive differently. We have to persuade the former that they should not lose occasions for doing good by putting it off, and we must counsel the latter not to lose their reward by heedlessly anticipating the time for doing good.

We have to make the indolent realize that in general, when we choose not to do what we are able to do, we cannot do it later when we want to. If the slothful are not aroused by fervor of an appropriate kind, torpor imperceptibly gains strength, and they lose all their desire for doing good. Solomon aptly observes that "indolence brings on deep sleep."[1] The indolent, in that their senses function correctly, we may call awake, though they grow torpid by doing nothing; their indolence is said to bring deep sleep because they gradually lose their wakefulness and their ability to sense things correctly as their inclination to do good ceases.

The text continues, "and a careless person will suffer hunger."[2] When people neglect themselves, not directing their energies upward, they are liable to desire what is low; when they do not pull themselves together by zeal for the heights they are wounded by a hunger for the depths. Thus as they are not concerned to constrain themselves by discipline, in their hunger they dissipate themselves in a desire

---

1. Prov. 19:15.
2. Ibid.

for pleasure. So Solomon, again, says, "The idle are given entirely to desires." Truth himself proclaims that when a single spirit goes out of a house we call it clean, but while it is empty that spirit returns with many more and regains possession.[3]

As the indolent are neglecting to do what they should do they often propose to themselves certain difficulties and heedlessly indulge their fears. As though coming across something that might reasonably cause them anxiety, they show that their idleness and inactivity are not unreasonable. Solomon rightly says to them, "Because of the cold the indolent would not plow; in the summer they will beg, and nothing will be given them."[4] The indolent do not plow because of the cold when slothful torpor holds them and they find an excuse for not doing the good they ought to do. The indolent do not plow because of the cold when they leave important actions undone out of their fear of the little evils that confront them.

Rightly then does he say that "in the summer they will beg, and nothing will be given them." Those who do not labor now in doing good will vainly ask for access to the kingdom when the burning sun of judgment appears; they will receive nothing in the summer when they beg. Again, Solomon rightly says of them, "Whoever observes the wind does not sow, and whoever regards the clouds never reaps."[5] What does the wind represent but temptation by evil spirits? And what do clouds moved by the wind symbolize if not opposition by the wicked? Clouds are driven by the winds because the wicked are aroused by blasts from unclean spirits. "Whoever observes the wind does not sow," therefore, "and whoever regards the clouds never reaps," because those who fear temptation by evil spirits and persecution by the wicked neither sow the seed of

---

3. Prov. 13:4, a literal translation of the Septuagint; Matt. 12:44-45.
4. Prov. 20:4.
5. Eccl. 11:4.

good works in the present nor cut the sheaves of a holy recompense hereafter.

On the other hand, the impulsive spoil their good deeds when they anticipate their time; while failing to discern the good they often rush headlong into evil. They give no thought to what to do, or when to do it, but usually recognize that they ought not to have done something after they have done it. Solomon says to such people, as to a disciple, "My child, do nothing without deliberation, and when it is done you will not regret it," and again, "Let your eyes precede your steps."[6] Eyes precede steps when good counsel anticipates action. Those who neglect to look ahead by reflecting on what they are about to do set out, they close their eyes, and they advance on their way, but as they are not looking at what is in front of them they quickly fall to the ground. They do not consider with the eye of deliberation where they ought to set down the foot of action.

---

6. Sirach 32:19; Prov. 4:25.

16

The Meek and the Irascible

W E MUST COUNSEL the meek and the irascible differently. Sometimes when the meek exercise authority they suffer from torpor and sloth, which are near neighbors to meekness. They frequently relax the rigor of severity beyond what is necessary by indulging too much gentleness. On the other hand, when the irascible assume a position of authority their anger impels them into a fit of rage; they disturb their subordinates' lives by destroying their tranquillity and peace. When fury drives them to the brink, they do not know what they are doing, and no more do they know what they are suffering from themselves. Sometimes, however, and this is more serious, they regard the anger that goads them on as righteous zeal; when we take vice for virtue the guilt piles up even as we feel no anxiety. The meek, then, frequently grow torpid from tedium and inactivity, while the irascible are frequently deceived by the zeal of rectitude. The former unconsciously add vice to virtue, while the latter take their vice to be a burning virtue.

We must counsel the former to avoid what is near them, and the latter to pay attention to what is in them; the former to discern what they lack, and the latter what they have. The meek must embrace their responsibility, and the irascible must condemn their disorder. We must counsel the meek to strive to become partisans of righteousness, and the irascible to add meekness to the zeal they imagine that they have. This is why the Holy Spirit has been revealed to us in a dove and in fire.[1] The Spirit causes all those it fills to be meek with the simplicity of the dove, and burning with the fire of zeal. None of those who sacrifice either their fervent zeal to the tranquillity that meekness brings, or their meekness to burning zeal, are filled with the Holy Spirit.

Perhaps we can see this better if we bring out Paul's teaching. To two disciples who were gifted with the same love he gave different advice with regard to their preaching. Counseling Timothy he said, "Reprove, entreat, rebuke with utmost patience and doctrine," and counseling Titus, "Declare these things, exhort and reprove with all authority."[2]

When dispensing his teaching with such skill, why did he urge authority on the one and patience on the other, unless Titus appeared to him too meek, and Timothy a little too impetuous? He was arousing the former to greater zeal, and tempering the latter with gentleness and patience. He was adding to Titus what was lacking, and taking from Timothy what was too much. He was spurring Titus on, and checking Timothy. The great husbandman of the church of which he had the charge watered some of the sprouts so that they would grow, and he cut back others when he saw that they were growing out of bounds.[3] Otherwise, those not growing might bear no fruit, and those growing immoderately would lose what they put forth.

The anger that steals upon us in the guise of zeal, and the anger that troubles an unquiet heart without pretext of righteousness, are entirely different. The former extends beyond where it should be, while the latter is always enkindled where it should not be. We have to realize that the irascible differ from the impatient in this, that the latter do not tolerate what others do to them, while the former cause

---

1. Matt. 3:16; Acts 2:3–4.
2. 2 Tim. 4:2; Titus 2:15.
3. 1 Cor. 3:6–9.

what others have to tolerate. The irascible often pursue even those who try to avoid them, provoking quarrels, and enjoying the distress caused by confrontation.

Our rebukes are more effective if we avoid making them when people are actually stirred up by their anger. Once aroused, they are not aware of what they are hearing, but when they are restored to themselves they listen more willingly to words of exhortation in proportion to their shame at having been calmly tolerated. To a person drunk on rage every right word seems wrong. We praise Abigail for saying nothing to Nabal about his offense while he was drunk, and for bringing it up when he had slept off the wine.[4] He was able to recognize the evil he had done precisely because he did not hear of it when drunk.

When the irascible attack others in such a way that these cannot get away from them, they should not be reproached openly, but treated cautiously, with a certain deference. We can show this better by bringing up Abner's deed. Scripture says that when Asahel attacked him with inconsiderate haste, "Abner said to Asahel, 'Turn back, do not follow me, so that I will not have to pierce you to the ground.' He refused to listen, and would not turn away. So Abner struck him in the groin with the butt of his spear and ran him through, and he died."[5]

What kind of person was Asahel if not one of those whose rage bursts out violently and leads them to the brink? The more outrageously these people are carried away, the more carefully must we avoid them in their rage. Thus Abner—whose name means "lamp of the father"[6]— fled from Asahel. When teachers, whose tongues reveal God's heavenly light, see that someone is being borne along the precipice of rage, and yet manage to avoid exchanging words with such an angry person, they are like

---

4. 1 Sam. 25:36–37.
5. 2 Sam. 2:22–23.
6. Jerome *Liber interp. Hebr. nominum* 34.16.

one unwilling to strike a pursuer. But when nothing appeases the irascible, when, like Asahel, they do not cease pursuing and raving, those trying to check their frenzy must not on any account let themselves be aroused to anger—they must show all the calm they can. They must simply bring forth something to pierce the angry person indirectly.

Thus when Abner stood against his pursuer he pierced him not with the blade but with the butt of his spear. To thrust with the point is to oppose with an open rebuke. To strike a pursuer with the butt of the spear is in some way to touch the raging person quietly, and to overcome by sparing. Asahel sank down on the spot—when agitated people feel that they are being spared, and yet are touched calmly in their depths by a reasonable response, they fall down at once from the pitch they had reached. Those who recoil from their frenzy when struck by gentleness die, as it were, without a spear.

17

The Humble and the Proud

W E MUST COUNSEL the humble and the proud differently. We must make the former understand that the excellence they possess by hope is true; we must convey to the latter that the temporal glory they do not possess even when they have it in their grasp is nothing. The humble must hear that what they are seeking is eternal and what they scorn is transitory; the proud must hear that they are striving for transitory things and squandering those that are eternal.

Let the humble listen to the authoritative voice of Truth: "All who humble themselves will be exalted," and let the proud hear that "all who exalt themselves will be humbled." The humble must hear that "humility goes before honor," and the proud that "a haughty spirit goes before a fall." Let the humble hear, "To whom will I look if not to one humble and quiet, who trembles at my word?" and the proud, "How can dust and ashes be proud?" Let the humble hear that "God regards the lowly," and the proud that "the haughty he knows from afar." Let the humble hear that "the Son of Man came not to be served but to serve," and the proud that "pride is the beginning of all sin." Let the humble hear that our Redeemer "humbled himself, and became obedient to the point of death," and the proud hear what is written of their chief: "He is king over all the children of pride."[1] The devil's pride became the occasion of our ruin,

---

1. Luke 18:14; Prov. 15:33; 16:18; Isa. 66:2; Sirach 10:9; Ps. 138:6; Matt. 20:28; Sirach 10:13; Phil. 2:8; Job 41:34.

and God's humility has been the means of our redemption. Our enemy, created one among all things, wanted to appear exalted above all things; our Redeemer, while remaining great above all things, deigned to become little among all things.

We should say, then, to the humble, that when they abase themselves they ascend toward likeness to God, and to the proud, that when they exalt themselves they fall into imitation of the apostate angel. What is baser than pride? When it overreaches it distances itself from the true heights. And what is more sublime than humility? When it debases itself to the depth it unites itself to its creator, who remains above all that is.

We must carefully consider something else about these people. Some often delude themselves by an appearance of humility, and some are deceived by an ignorance of their own pride. Those who seem to themselves humble often experience an anxiety they ought not to feel with regard to other human beings, while the proud are usually too free in their speech. When they are required to correct certain vices, the former refrain out of fear while supposing that they are keeping silent out of humility, and the latter speak up with the impatience that comes from their pride, while supposing that they are speaking with the freedom that comes from being right. The fault of timidity under a show of humility keeps the humble from rebuking waywardness, whereas impetuous self-conceit in the guise of freedom impels the proud to censure when they should not, or more than they should.

We must counsel the proud, then, that their freedom has limits, and the humble that their submissiveness can go too far. The former are not to turn their defense of justice into an exercise in pride, and the latter, as they strive to be more submissive to people than is required, should not force themselves to respect even their vices.

But we must take into account that we often reprimand the proud to better effect if we mix with our criticisms a certain amount of conciliatory praise. We should mention some of their good qualities, or some they could have if they lack them now. When this has disposed them to listen peacefully, then we have an opportunity to cut away the bad qualities we dislike. We begin by touching an unbroken horse gently so that afterward we can train it completely, even by using a whip. We add honey to bitter medicine so that what is good for our health will not taste bad—while the sweetness deceives the taste, the bitterness purges us. So in the first words of our reprimand of the proud we must mix in a proportionate amount of praise; then, as they admit the compliments that they like, they may also accept the corrections that they hate.

In general, we can better persuade the proud of what is advantageous if we tell them that their progress benefits us more than it does them, and if we ask them to amend their lives for our sake rather than for their own. Pride is easily turned to good if the turning is believed to benefit others as well. When Moses, with God guiding him, was making his march through the desert, led by the pillar of cloud, he wanted to draw his kinsman Hobab away from his pagan surroundings and bring him under the rule of almighty God. He said to him, "We are setting out for the place the Lord will give us. Come with us, and we will treat you well, for the Lord has promised good to Israel." When Hobab replied, "I will not go with you, but I will go back to my own land where I was born," Moses immediately added, "Do not leave us, for you know where we should camp in the wilderness, and you will be our guide."[2]

Moses was not anxious because he didn't know the way. His acquaintance with God had given him prophetic knowledge—outwardly the pillar was preceding him, and inwardly he was being instructed through familiar conversation with God concerning everything. But when he was addressing a proud listener, the farsighted man asked him to

---

2. Num. 10:29–31.

give his assistance; he was looking for a guide on the journey in order that he might become his guide toward life. Moses made his proud listener as devoted to his urging toward a better life as he judged himself needed; Hobab believed that he would be leading the one who was exhorting him, and agreed to his words of exhortation.

18

The Stubborn and the Fickle

W E MUST COUNSEL the stubborn and the fickle differently. We must tell the former that they think themselves more than they are, and so do not accept the advice of others; we must make the latter understand that they neglect and undervalue themselves, and for this reason they change their opinions lightly from moment to moment. We must tell the former that if they did not think themselves better than other people they would not prefer their own counsel to everyone else's; we must tell the latter that if they gave any consideration at all to what they are, the changing winds would not turn them in so many different directions.

To the stubborn Paul says, "Do not be wise in your own eyes," but the fickle, in contrast, hear him say, "Let us not be tossed around by every wind of doctrine." Solomon says of the former, "They shall eat the fruit of their own way, and be sated with their own devices," and of the latter he writes, "The hearts of fools will be inconsistent."[1] The hearts of the wise are always consistent because, as they accept good advice, they are continually guided toward good. The hearts of fools are inconsistent because, in their instability, they never remain what they were.

As some faults engender others, as it were, spontaneously, so some arise out of others. We must by all means be aware that our corrections are most effective when we dry

---

1. Rom. 12:16; Eph. 4:14; Prov. 1:31; 15:7.

up their bitter source. Stubbornness comes from pride, fickleness from light-mindedness.

We must then counsel the stubborn that they have to acknowledge their pride and aim at overcoming themselves. Otherwise, while they outwardly scorn to be influenced by the good advice of others, they may be inwardly held captive by pride. We must counsel them to consider carefully that the Son of Man, whose will is always one with the Father's, gave us an example of how we can subdue our wills when he said, "I do not seek my own will, but the will of the Father who sent me." To commend this virtue still more, he tells us beforehand that he will keep it in the last judgment: "I can do nothing on my own, but, as I hear, I judge."[2] With what conscience then can people disdain to accept the will of another when the Son of God and of Man affirms that when he comes to reveal the glory of his power he will not judge on his own?

On the other hand, we must counsel the fickle to strengthen their seriousness of purpose. When they cut out of their hearts the root of light-mindedness they dry up the fruits of instability; when they provide a solid place on which to lay a foundation they can then construct a strong building. We can only overcome fickleness if we first guard against light-mindedness. Paul testified that he was free of this when he said, "Have I been light-minded? Do I make my plans according to human standards so that there is in me 'yes' and 'no'?"[3] He means, "I am not moved by the changing winds because I do not yield to the vice of light-mindedness."

---

2. John 5:30; 6:38.
3. 2 Cor. 1:17.

19

The Gluttonous
and the Abstemious

W E MUST COUNSEL the gluttonous and the abstemious differently. We find talking too much, lack of seriousness, and debauchery in the former, and faults, sometimes of impatience, sometimes of pride, in the latter. Unless immoderate speech carried away the gluttonous, the rich man—who, we are told, feasted sumptuously every day—would not have been so severely burned in his tongue. His words were, "Father Abraham, have mercy on me, and send Lazarus to dip the tip of his finger in water to cool my tongue, for I am in agony in this flame."[1] These words show us that by his daily feasting he sinned frequently with his tongue—while he was burning all over, he especially longed for cooling in his tongue.

The sacred authority testifies that lack of seriousness follows gluttony: "The people sat down to eat and drink, and rose up to revel." Gluttony frequently draws us to debauchery because the excess that distends the stomach arouses the stings of lust. For this reason the divine voice told our cunning enemy, who gave life to the first human being's sensuality in the desire for fruit and bound him in the snares of sin, "You will crawl on your breast and your belly."[2] This means, "You will dominate human hearts by thought and gluttony."

---

1. Luke 16:19, 24.
2. Exod. 32:6; Gen. 3:14.

The prophet testifies that debauchery accompanies the gluttonous, concealing his meaning in a story, when he says, "The chief of the cooks broke down the walls of Jerusalem."[3] The belly is chief of the cooks; cooks pay it great respect—they fill it pleasurably with food. The walls of Jerusalem are the virtues of the soul, raised in a desire for heavenly peace. The chief of the cooks throws down the walls of Jerusalem because, while gluttony distends the belly, debauchery destroys the virtues of the soul.

On the other hand, unless impatience frequently deprived the abstemious of their inner tranquillity, when Peter said, "Support your faith with virtue, virtue with knowledge, and knowledge with self-control," he would not have immediately and deliberately added, "and self-control with patience." He foresaw that the abstemious would lack patience, and advised them to acquire it. Again, unless the fault of pride sometimes entered the minds of the abstemious, Paul would not have said, "Those who abstain must not pass judgment on those who eat." And again, speaking to others, and alluding to the precepts of those who boasted of the virtue of abstinence, he said, "These have an appearance of wisdom in promoting superstition and self-abasement and not sparing the body, but they are of no value against physical indulgence."[4]

In this connection we should note that the great preacher links a show of humility to superstition in his argument. When abstinence weakens the flesh more than is necessary, outwardly humility appears, but inwardly pride grows strong because of this very humility. If people were not at times inflated by the virtue of abstinence, the arrogant Pharisee would not have counted it among his great merits: "I fast twice a week."[5]

---

3. 2 Kings 25:10; Jer. 52:12. Gregory's text agrees with the Septuagint; the Vulgate has *militum*, troops, rather than *coquorum*, cooks.

4. 2 Peter 1:5–6; Rom. 14:3; Col. 2:23.

5. Luke 18:12.

We must then counsel the gluttonous not to pierce themselves with the sword of debauchery when they abandon themselves to the pleasures of the table. They should see how they are threatened by talkativeness and light-mindedness through eating; if they do not, as they pleasure their bellies they may be more painfully caught in the toils of vice. We stray farther from the second Adam when, by stretching out our hands immoderately for food, we repeat the fall of the first.[6]

On the other hand, we must counsel the abstemious to take care never to bring more consuming vices to birth while they avoid gluttony, as if out of their virtue. Otherwise, while they chasten their flesh they may break out in impatience. Subduing the flesh is no virtue if anger overcomes the heart! At times, however, when the abstemious repress their anger, some, as it were, exotic source of delight comes along and corrupts them; then, as they fail to preserve themselves from vices of the spirit, their abstinence loses its value.

Therefore the prophet rightly remarks that "on your fast days you serve your own pleasure," and then "you quarrel and fight while you fast, and you strike out with your fists."[7] Pleasure corresponds to delight, and the fist to anger. In vain do we weaken our bodies through abstinence if our hearts are brought down by uncontrollable emotions and destroyed by vices.

Again, we must counsel them to preserve their abstinence continually and without wavering, and never to consider this virtue extraordinary in the eyes of our hidden judge. If they do otherwise, if they believe it to be exceptionally meritorious, their hearts may become proud. The prophet asks, "Is this the fast that I have chosen? Instead, share your bread with the hungry, and bring the homeless poor into your house." In this connection we should reflect on how little

---

6. See 1 Cor. 15:45, 47.

7. Isa. 58:3–4—perhaps quoted from memory.

we are to value abstinence when it is not recommended by other virtues. Hence Joel tells us, "Sanctify a fast."[8] To sanctify a fast is to make physical abstinence worthy of God by adding other virtues to it.

We must counsel the abstemious that their offering of abstinence pleases God when they bestow the provisions they take from themselves on the needy. They must listen carefully to what the Lord charges through the prophet: "When you fasted and lamented in the fifth month and in the seventh for these seventy years, was it for me that you fasted? And when you eat and when you drink, do you not eat for yourselves and drink for yourselves?"[9] People fast for themselves and not for God when, instead of giving it to the needy, they keep for their bellies later what for a time they deny them.

To prevent their appetite for food from throwing some people off their guard, and their mortified flesh from tripping up others through pride, let the gluttonous listen to Truth himself: "Be on guard so that your hearts are not weighed down with dissipation and drunkenness and the worries of this life." To this he adds a helpful source of fear: "and that day come upon you unexpectedly. Like a trap it will come upon all who live on the face of the whole earth." Let the abstemious hear that "what goes into the mouth does not defile a person, but what comes out of the mouth defiles a person." Let the former hear that "food is meant for the stomach, and the stomach for God, and God destroys both one and the other," and again, "not in reveling and drunkenness," and again, that "food does not commend us to God." Let the latter hear, "To the pure all things are pure, but to the corrupt and unbelieving nothing is pure." Let the former hear, "Their god is the belly, and their glory is in their shame." Let the latter hear, "Some will forsake the faith," and then, that "they forbid marriage and

---

8. Isa. 58:5, 7; Joel 2:15.
9. Zech. 7:5–6.

demand abstinence from foods which God created to be received with thanksgiving by those who believe and know the truth." Let the former hear, "It is good not to eat meat or drink wine or do anything that makes your brother or sister stumble." Let the latter hear, "Take a little wine for your stomach and your frequent ailments."[10] All this is so that the gluttonous may learn not to have an inordinate desire for the food of the flesh, and the abstemious may not dare to condemn God's creation, for which they have no desire.

---

10. Luke 21:34–35; Matt. 15:11; 1 Cor. 6:13; Rom. 13:13; 1 Cor. 8:8; Titus 1:15; Phil. 3:19; 1 Tim. 4:1, 3; Rom. 14:21; 1 Tim. 5:23.

20

The Generous and the Grasping

WE MUST COUNSEL DIFFERENTLY those who already give away their possessions out of compassion, and those who strive to seize even what belongs to others. We must counsel those who already give away their possessions out of compassion not to raise themselves arrogantly above those on whom they bestow earthly things. They should not reckon themselves superior to others because they see themselves supporting them. Those in charge of an earthly establishment assign the ranks and duties of those in their charge, appointing some to manage, and others to be managed. They order the former to provide what is necessary, and the latter to receive it from them. Frequently, however, managers give offense, while those who are managed remain in the good graces of the one in charge—those who give direction to others draw wrath on themselves, and those who live by the direction of others go on without causing offense.

We must then counsel those who already give away what they possess out of compassion to recognize that the Lord of heaven has put them in a position to provide others with their temporal means of subsistence. They must do this humbly, out of their understanding that what they are dispensing is not their own. When they consider that they have been appointed to serve the people on whom they are bestowing what they have themselves received, they will not swell up with pride, but rather deflate from fear.

They must take care not to distribute what has been entrusted to them unworthily. They must not give to those who should get nothing, or keep back from those who should get something, or give much to those who should get little, or little to those who should get much; they should not scatter what they are giving uselessly by haste, or torment those who ask of them harmfully by delays; they should not let the thought of receiving a favor in return sneak in, or let a craving for ephemeral honors extinguish the luminous act of giving; no sadness should accompany the act of offering, nor should they become giddy over an offering well made. Then, when everything has been carried out as it ought to be, they should not attribute anything to themselves, and so lose at once everything they have accomplished.

To keep them from attributing their virtue of generosity to themselves let them listen to Scripture: "Whoever serves must do so with the strength that God supplies." So that they will not rejoice immoderately in their good deeds let them hear, "When you have done all that you were ordered to do, say, 'We are worthless servants; we have done what we ought to do.'" To keep sadness from spoiling their liberality let them hear that "God loves a cheerful giver." That they may not seek ephemeral honors as a result of their gifts let them listen to Scripture: "Do not let your left hand know what your right hand is doing"—that is, never mingle renown in this present life with your holy task, but let your righteous deeds remain ignorant of your craving for compliments. To keep them from looking for a return from a favor they are bestowing let them listen to Scripture: "When you give a lunch or a dinner, do not invite your friends, or your brothers and sisters, or your relatives, or your rich neighbors, in case they should invite you in return, and you should be repaid. When you give a banquet, invite the poor, the cripples, the lame and the blind, and you will be blessed, because they cannot repay you."[1]

---

1. 1 Pet. 4:11; Luke 17:10; 2 Cor. 9:7; Matt. 6:3; Luke 14:12–14.

To keep them from giving late what they should give quickly, let them listen to Scripture: "Do not say to your friend, 'Go, and come again, and tomorrow I will give to you,' when you are able to give at once."[2] So that they will not uselessly scatter what they possess under pretext of liberality let them hear, "Let your alms sweat in your hand."[3] So that they will not give little when much is needed, let them hear, "One who sows sparingly will also reap sparingly." To keep them from giving away great amounts when they should give little—so that they afterward suffer scarcity and burst out in impatience—let them listen to Scripture: "There should not be relief for others and trouble for you, but a fair balance; your abundance can supply their need, so that their abundance may also supply your need."[4] When givers who cannot endure scarcity take too much away from themselves, they are looking for occasions for impatience with themselves. They must first prepare themselves to be patient—then they can give away large amounts, or even everything. Otherwise, when scarcity attacks them they do not bear it with equanimity, they lose their reward for their former liberality, and their subsequent complaining causes them much harm.

To keep them from giving nothing at all to those to whom they should give a little let them listen to Scripture: "Give to everyone who asks of you." So that they will not give something, however little, to those to whom they should give nothing let them hear, "Give to the good, but do not receive a sinner. Do good to the humble, but do not give to the ungodly," and again, "Place your bread and wine on the grave of the righteous, but do not eat and drink of it with sinners."[5] Those who give assistance to evildoers

---

2. Prov. 3:28.

3. Source unknown, but quoted as scriptural in *Didache* 1.6, and by Augustine et al.

4. 2 Cor. 9:6; 8:13–14.

5. Luke 6:30; Sirach 12:4–5; Tob. 4:17.

because they are evildoers are offering their bread and wine to sinners. Thus some of the rich in this world support entertainers with great liberality, while Christ's poor are tormented by hunger. Those, however, who give their bread to the needy, even though they are sinners—not because they are sinners, but because they are human beings—are not supporting sinners but the righteous poor; they love in them not their fault but their nature.

We must also counsel those who already give away their possessions out of compassion to take care not to commit sins that need atonement while they are atoning by their alms for those they have committed. They should not imagine that God's righteousness is for sale, thinking that they can sin with impunity if only they take care to give money for their sins. "Life is more than food, and the body is more than clothing."[6] Those who bestow food and clothing on the poor, but nevertheless defile their own souls or bodies with wickedness, are making a smaller offering to righteousness and a larger one to sin; they have given their possessions to God, and themselves to the devil.

On the other hand, we must counsel those whose intention is to seize even what belongs to others to listen carefully to what the Lord says when he comes in judgment: "I was hungry and you gave me no food, I was thirsty and you gave me nothing to drink, I was a stranger and you did not welcome me, naked and you gave me no clothing, sick and in prison and you did not visit me." He tells these people to "depart from me, you that are accursed, into the eternal fire prepared for the devil and his angels."[7]

See how they do not hear that they have committed robbery or any other violent act—and yet they are delivered up to the eternal fires of hell! We can gather the greatness of the condemnation visited on those who seize what belongs to others if those who unwisely hold on to what is their

---

6. Luke 12:23; Matt. 6:25.
7. Matt. 25:42–43, 41.

own suffer such punishment. If not giving brings so great a penalty, let them weigh the guilt brought upon them by stealing. If kindness not done brings so great a punishment, let them consider what injustice done deserves.

When these people are intent on seizing what belongs to others let them hear what Scripture says: "Woe to you who heap up what is not your own! How long will you load yourselves with thick mud?" For the covetous, to load themselves with thick mud is to pile up earthly riches with a burden of sin. When they desire to add greatly to their living space let them hear, "Woe to you who join house to house, who add field to field, until there is no place left. Will you alone live in the midst of the land?" This is to ask, "How far do you extend yourselves, you who must have companions in a common world? You oppress your neighbors, and you are forever finding people at whose expense you can extend yourselves." Let those who aspire to increase their wealth hear, "The covetous will not be satisfied with money, and those who love riches will not gather their fruits."[8] They would gather their fruits if they were willing to distribute them, without loving them. Those who love them and do not let them go will leave them here behind, fruitless.

When people are burning to be filled with all riches at once they should hear what Scripture says: "One who is in a hurry to be rich will not be blameless."[9] Those ambitious to increase their wealth are not concerned to avoid sin. They are caught as birds are—while looking greedily at the bait of earthly things, they are not aware of the noose of sin that strangles them.

When they crave the advantages of the present world, no matter which ones, and are unaware of the losses they will suffer in the world to come, let them listen to Scripture: "An inheritance quickly acquired in the beginning will be

---

8. Hab. 2:6; Isa. 5:8; Eccl. 5:9.
9. Prov. 28:20.

without a blessing in the end." In this life we form our beginning so that at the end we may come to share in a blessing. Those people who are quick to acquire an inheritance in the beginning cut themselves off from a share in a blessing at the end; while they are seeking increase here through their wicked greed, they become disinherited from their eternal patrimony hereafter. Let those whose ambition is great, and who are able to satisfy all their ambition, hear, "What does it profit people to gain the whole world, but bring about the loss of their lives?"[10] This is as if Truth were asking openly, "What does it profit people to amass everything that is outside themselves, and lose only this, themselves?"

Frequently a speedier way to correct the covetousness of those who seize what belongs to others is for a counselor to tell them how fleeting is this present life; to remind them of the long time some people have spent in trying to become rich in this world, people unable to rest long in the riches they had acquired; how a speedy death took from them suddenly and at once everything they had amassed by their wickedness, neither at once, nor suddenly; and how they left behind everything that they had seized, but took with them to the judgment the responsibility for seizing it. Let them listen to these instances of people whom they would doubtless themselves condemn by their words; then, when they return from their words to their hearts, they may at least be ashamed to imitate those whom they are judging.

---

10. Prov. 20:21; Matt. 16:26.

21

The Stingy and the Extravagant

WE MUST COUNSEL DIFFERENTLY those who neither desire others' goods nor give away their own, and those who give away what they have while constantly seizing what belongs to others. We must counsel those who neither desire others' goods nor give away their own that they should be well aware that the earth from which they were taken is common to all human beings, and in consequence provides support for everyone in common. In vain do those who claim God's common gift as their own private one reckon themselves guiltless. When they do not give away what they have received, they bring about their neighbor's death; nearly every day they are destroying those of the dying poor whose means of support they keep for themselves. We are not bestowing on the indigent poor what is ours when we supply them with what they need, but we are handing over what is their own. We are paying a debt of justice, not accomplishing a work of mercy.

Truth himself, when cautioning us concerning showing mercy, tells us, "Take care not to perform your justice before people." In agreement with him the psalmist says, "They have distributed freely, they have given to the poor; their justice endures forever." He prefers not to speak of mercy but of justice in connection with donations to the poor—it is surely just that those who receive what our common

Lord bestows should employ it for the common good. So Solomon says, "The just give, and will not hold back."[1]

We must also counsel them to consider carefully that the strict gardener makes the complaint against the fruitless fig tree that it even takes up the ground.[2] The fruitless fig tree takes up the ground when the stingy hold unprofitably what could benefit many; the fruitless fig tree takes up the ground when fools cover with the shade of their sloth a place that another could cultivate in the sunshine of a good deed.

But these people sometimes say, "We use what has been granted us, we don't look for what belongs to others. If we don't perform an act of mercy worth being rewarded, still we do nothing wrong." They feel this way because they have shut the ears of their hearts against the words of heaven. We are not shown that the rich man in the gospel, who was dressed in purple and fine linen and who feasted sumptuously every day, had seized what belongs to others, but that he employed what was his own fruitlessly.[3] Avenging hell received him after this life, not because he did anything unlawful, but because he gave himself up to what was lawful immoderately.

We must counsel the stingy to acknowledge that they do God this first injury when they return no sacrifice of mercy to the one who has given them everything. The psalmist says, "They will not give God their ransom, nor the price of redemption for their life." To give the price of redemption is to give back a good deed in return for the grace that has preceded it. John the Baptist cried out, "Even now the ax is lying at the root of the trees; every tree that does not bear good fruit will be cut down and thrown into the fire."[4] Those who think themselves blameless because they do not seize what belongs to others must look out for the

---

1. Matt. 6:1; Ps. 112:9; Prov. 21:26.
2. Luke 13:7.
3. Luke 16:19.
4. Ps. 49:7–8; Luke 3:9.

stroke of an ax near at hand. They should put off the torpor of shortsighted security; if they do not do this, when they neglect to bear the fruit of a good work they will be utterly cut off from the present life as if from their living roots.

On the other hand, we must counsel those who give away their possessions while constantly seizing what belongs to others not to crave an appearance of lavish generosity, and that their outward show of goodness makes them all the worse. When they give of their own without discretion these people do not fall into the complaints of impatience I mentioned earlier; when they are constrained by neediness they pass on into avarice. What is more unfortunate than the state of mind of those whose avarice is born of their generosity, and a harvest of sins is, as it were, sown by virtue? We must first counsel these people to learn how to hold on to their own possessions in a rational way, and then that they must not go after those of others. Unless the root of the fault is burned in its time of propagation, the thorns of avarice, growing luxuriant on the branches, will never wither. If we can establish the right of owning, we withdraw the occasion for plundering.

Then those we counsel must hear how they are to give of what they have with compassion—when, that is, they have learned not to mix their good deeds of mercy with the evil of robbery. They exact by violence what they give by compassion. To show mercy on account of sins is one thing; to sin on account of showing mercy is another—though this can no longer be called mercy, because what is embittered by the sap rising from a poisonous root does not develop into sweet fruit.

That is why the Lord, speaking through the prophet, even goes so far as to reject sacrifices: "I the Lord love justice, and I hate robbery with a burnt offering." Again, he says, "The sacrifices of the wicked are an abomination, for they are offered with evil intent." These people often steal from the needy what they give to God. Through a sage the

Lord reveals the great antipathy with which he rejects them: "Like one who kills a child before its parent's eyes is the person who offers a sacrifice from the property of the poor."[5] What could be more unbearable than the death of a child before its parent's eyes? God's great anger with regard to this kind of sacrifice is revealed by the comparison with the grief of a bereaved parent who has been deprived of a child.

These people often weigh the amount they give, but do not trouble to consider the amount they seize. They reckon what they have coming to them, but refuse to compute their faults. Let them listen to Scripture: "You who have collected wages have put them in a bag with holes."[6] People see the money when they pour it into a bag with holes, but not when it pours out. Those who pay attention to what they give, but do not consider how much they seize, are putting their wages into a bag with holes; they see them as they heap them up in hope of security, but do not see them as they lose them.

---

5. Isa. 61:8; Prov. 21:27; Sirach 34:24.
6. Hag. 1:6.

22

The Quarrelsome
and the Peaceable

W E MUST COUNSEL the quarrelsome and the
peaceable differently. We must counsel the quarrelsome that however virtuous they may be, they
are incapable of becoming spiritual persons if they do not
join themselves in concord with their neighbors. Scripture
tells us that "the fruit of the Spirit is love, joy, peace." Those
unconcerned to preserve the peace are refusing to bring
forth the fruit of the Spirit. Hence Paul asks, "While you
have jealously and quarreling among you, are you not of the
flesh?" Again, he tells us to "pursue peace with everyone,
and the holiness without which no one will see God." And
again, he admonishes us to "make every effort to maintain
the unity of the Spirit in the bond of peace: one body and
one spirit, as you were called in the one hope of your calling."[1] We never attain the one hope of our calling unless we
hasten toward it in a union of heart with our neighbors.

People who have received special gifts often lose the
greater gift of concord owing to their pride; those who
subdue their flesh more than others by restraining their
desire for food may disdain to be in concord with those
they surpass in abstinence. Those who separate abstinence
from concord should ponder the psalmist's advice to "praise
God with timbrel and choir."[2] The dry skin of the timbrel

---

1. Gal. 5:22; 1 Cor. 3:3; Heb. 12:14; Eph. 4:3–4.
2. Ps. 150:4.

resounds when struck, while the voices of a choir unite in concord. Those who mortify their bodies while leaving aside concord do indeed praise God with the timbrel, but not with the choir.

Greater knowledge frequently exalts some, and they dissociate themselves from others—as if the wiser they are, the more unwisely do they lose the virtue of concord! Let them listen to what Truth himself tells us: "Have salt in yourselves, and be at peace with one another."[3] Salt without peace is not a gift of virtue but evidence of condemnation. The better people's knowledge, the worse their failure—they will deserve punishment without excuse, because they had enough common sense to avoid sin if only they had wished to do so.

James rightly says to such people, "If you have bitter envy and quarreling in your hearts, do not be boastful and false to the truth. Such wisdom does not come down from above, but is earthly, unspiritual, devilish. The wisdom from above is first pure, then peaceable"[4]—pure, because its ideas are chaste; peaceable, because not separated by pride from the company of its neighbors.

We must counsel those who are at variance to be aware that as long as they are out of harmony with their neighbors' love no good deed of theirs is a sacrifice to God. Scripture says, "If you are offering your gift at the altar and remember there that your brother or sister has something against you, leave your gift there in front of the altar, go first to be reconciled to your brother or sister, and then come and offer your gift."[5] This precept should cause us to consider how intolerable is the fault of those people whose offering is rejected. Since all evils are done away with by subsequent good, let us consider how great the evils of discord are, since, unless we eliminate them utterly, we can do no subsequent good.

---

3. Mark 9:50.
4. James 3:14–15, 17.
5. Matt. 5:23.

We must counsel the quarrelsome that if they fail to heed the heavenly commandments they must open their inner eyes to ponder what takes place among lower beings: birds of one and the same kind generally do not separate from one another but fly together in flocks, and brute animals graze in herds. If we think this over carefully, we see that irrational nature indicates through its concord how great an evil rational nature commits through discord when, by exercising reason, it loses what irrational nature retains by natural instinct.

On the other hand, we must counsel the peaceable not to be more attached than need be to the peace they possess, and so fail to desire to achieve the peace that endures. Tranquil circumstances are frequently a serious temptation. As a result, the less troubled they are in their present state, the less attractive is what calls them out, and the more they delight in what is present, the less do they seek what is eternal. When distinguishing earthly peace from heavenly, and summoning his disciples from present peace to the peace that is to come, Truth said, "My peace I leave you, my peace I give to you."[6] He means, "I leave behind a transitory peace, I give a peace that lasts." Hearts attached to the peace that is left behind never attain the peace that is to be given. We must hold the peace we now possess as something both to love and to spurn; if we love it inordinately, we who love it may be trapped in sin.

And so we must counsel the peaceable that as long as they have an excessive desire for human peace they may fail to condemn people's evil ways. When they connive at wrongdoing they dissociate themselves from their creator's peace; when they are afraid to deal publicly with human disputes they may be punished by the rupture of their inner covenant. What is transitory peace if not a sort of trace of eternal peace? What could be more foolish than to love a trace impressed in the dust, but not to love the one who impressed it?

---

6. John 14:27.

When David was binding himself totally to a covenant of inner peace he claimed that he would have no concord with the wicked: "Have I not hated those who hate you, O God, and wasted away because of your enemies? I have hated them with perfect hatred; I counted them my enemies."[7] To hate God's enemies with perfect hatred is to love what they are and to censure what they do, to reprove the ways of the wicked and to improve their lives.

When we refrain from censuring others we must consider how great is the fault of keeping peace with bad people. The great prophet David offered to God in sacrifice his arousing against himself the enmity of the wicked on the Lord's behalf! When the tribe of Levi took up the sword and went back and forth throughout the camp, not sparing the sinners they were to smite, Scripture says that they consecrated their hands to God. When Phinehas rejected the favor of his sinful fellow citizens and struck those cohabiting with the Midianites, by his own anger he appeased the Lord's.[8]

Truth himself said, "Do not think that I have come to bring peace on the earth. I have not come to bring peace, but a sword." When we heedlessly associate ourselves in friendship with the wicked we bind ourselves to their faults. Jehoshaphat, who received so much praise for his earlier deeds, was rebuked as one about to perish for his friendly relations with King Ahab. The Lord said to him through the prophet, "You help the ungodly and join in friendship with those who hate the Lord. Because of this you deserve the Lord's wrath. Nevertheless, good works are found in you, for you destroyed the groves from the land of Judah."[9] Those whose lives are in harmony with wrongdoers through friendship are by that fact at variance with the one who is supremely righteous.

---

7. Ps. 139:21–22.
8. Exod. 32:26–29; Num. 25:7.
9. Matt. 10:34; 2 Chron. 19:2–3.

We must counsel the peaceable that they should not scruple to disturb their own temporal peace by bursting out in words of reproof. Again, we must counsel them to maintain within themselves by their undiminished love the peace they are disturbing outwardly by their aggressive words. David asserts that he prudently did both things when he says, "Among those who hate peace I was peaceable; when I spoke to them they attacked me without cause."[10] Do you see how when he spoke he was attacked, and yet when he was attacked he was peaceable? He neither ceased reproving those who were in a rage, nor failed to love those he was reproving.

Paul says, "If it is possible, so far as it depends on you, have peace with all."[11] When urging his disciples to have peace with all he begins by saying, "If it is possible," and then adds, "so far as it depends on you." Only with difficulty could they have peace with all if they were reprimanding evil deeds—but while our rebukes are disturbing the temporal peace of the hearts of the wicked, we must keep it inviolate in our own hearts. He is then right to say, "so far as it depends on you," meaning that since peace exists by the agreement of two parties, if it is driven off by those who are reprimanded, let it still be maintained undiminished in those who do the reprimanding.

Paul also gives this advice to his disciples: "Take note of those who do not obey what we say in this letter, and have nothing to do with them so that they may be ashamed," but he adds at once, "Do not regard them as enemies, but reprimand them as brothers and sisters."[12] He means, "Break the external peace between you, but protect your internal peace with them in your heart's core. Then your discord may so strike the sinners' minds that peace, even if they refuse it, does not depart from your own hearts."

---

10. Ps. 120:6–7.
11. Rom. 12:18.
12. 2 Thess. 3:14–15.

23

Sowers of Discord and Peacemakers

W E MUST COUNSEL DIFFERENTLY those who sow discord and those who make peace. We must counsel those who sow discord to recognize whose followers they are. Scripture says of the apostate angel who sowed weeds in the midst of a good crop, "An enemy has done this," and Solomon says of one of his partisans, "An apostate, an unprofitable man, goes around with crooked talk, winking his eyes, shuffling his feet, gesturing with his finger, with perverted heart devising evil, and continually sowing discord."[1]

Notice that the man Solomon chooses to call a sower of discord he first called an apostate. If that man had not, like the angel who became proud, first fallen away from his maker's sight by turning away in private, he would not afterward have reached the point of sowing discord in public. The man is rightly described as winking the eyes, gesturing with the finger, and shuffling the feet because inner vigilance keeps the members of the body outwardly in good order. Those who lose their spiritual equilibrium subsequently slip into a physical restlessness; they indicate by their outward agitation that they have no inner root to sustain them.

Sowers of discord should listen to the words of Scripture: "Blessed are the peacemakers, for they will be called children

---

1. Matt. 13:28; Prov. 6:12–14.

of God."[2] Let them grasp from the contrast that if those who make peace are called children of God, without any doubt those who disturb it are children of Satan. All those who cut themselves off by discord from the vigorous sap of love wither. Even though they bear the fruit of good deeds in their actions, these are nothing because they do not grow out of the unity of love.

Let sowers of discord consider well how they are multiplying their sins! By carrying out one wicked act they root out all the virtues at once from human hearts. By one evil they accomplish numberless evils, because by sowing discord they are extinguishing love, the mother of all the virtues. God reckons nothing more precious than the virtue of love, and the devil desires nothing more than the extinction of love. Those who destroy love of their neighbors by sowing discord become intimate servants of God's enemy. When he had lost love the devil fell; when these people take it away from wounded hearts they cut off their path of ascent.

On the other hand, we must counsel those who make peace not to deprive their great undertaking of its full value by failing to know those among whom they ought to establish peace. Disunity among the good causes much harm—unity among the wicked is much more harmful! If peace unites the crooked in their iniquity, their ability to do wrong gains strength; when they agree among themselves in wickedness, they can act together more energetically to torment the good.

Hence the divine voice addresses these words to blessed Job against the preachers of that condemned vessel, namely Antichrist: "The members of his flesh cling together." The partisans of Antichrist, represented by scales, are shown to be "one joined to another so that no air can pass between them."[3] Since his followers are not divided by disagreements among themselves, they form a more oppressive

---

2. Matt. 5:9.
3. Job 41:23, 16 (Vulg. 41:14, 7).

instrument for slaughtering the good. Those who associate with the wicked in peace give strength to wickedness because, as they are unanimous in their persecution, their oppression of the good is worse.

The illustrious preacher, Paul, was overtaken by fierce persecution from the Pharisees and the Sadducees. When he saw that they were firmly united against him, he tried to divide them among themselves by crying out, "Men, brothers, I am a Pharisee, the son of Pharisees. I am on trial concerning the hope and resurrection of the dead."[4] The Sadducees denied the hope and resurrection of the dead, while the Pharisees believed, in accordance with the teachings of the holy text. Paul broke up the unanimity of his persecutors, and with the crowd—which at first, when united, had fiercely harassed him—divided, he left unharmed.

And so we must counsel those engaged in making peace first to instill a love of inner peace in the hearts of wrongdoers so that later they may be able to experience the benefits of external peace. With their hearts engaged in recognizing the former, they will not be drawn to wickedness by attempting to grab the latter. While looking forward to heavenly peace, they should not in any way turn toward earthly peace to their own undoing.

When, however, wrongdoers are in no position to harm the good, even if they want to, we should bring about earthly peace among them even before they are capable of recognizing heavenly peace. Then, at the very least love of neighbor may soften those whose unholy malice hardens them against the love of God, and they may pass on toward something better as if from a point nearby, rising to what is far away from them, the peace of their creator.

---

4. Acts 23:6.

24

Interpreters of the Law

W E MUST COUNSEL DIFFERENTLY those who wrongly interpret the words of the holy law, and those who interpret them correctly but speak without humility. We must counsel those who wrongly interpret the words of the holy law to consider well that they are turning a most wholesome drink of wine into a potion that will poison them. They are inflicting a deadly wound on themselves with a surgical blade, using it to destroy what is sound in themselves instead of cutting away what is diseased, as they ought to do for their health's sake.

We must counsel them to consider that holy Scripture is like a lamp set out for them during the night of this present life. When they misinterpret it, the light turns into darkness. Of course their perverse attitude would not carry them away to a false understanding if they were not first puffed up with pride. While they reckon that they are wiser than others they scorn to follow anyone else to a better understanding. They try at all costs to discredit what these others have correctly understood, and to confirm their own perverse views, in order to squeeze out a reputation for knowledge among the uneducated.

The prophet has correctly said that "they have ripped open pregnant women in Gilead in order to enlarge their territory." Gilead means "the witness heap."[1] Because the

---

1. Amos 1:13; Gen. 31:48.

82

whole assembly of the church as one serves as a witness to the truth, we can rightly take Gilead to represent the church, which bears witness to the truth about God in the single voice of all the faithful. Souls are called pregnant when by divine love they conceive an understanding of the word; if they come to full term they will bring forth by the evidence of their deeds the understanding they have conceived.

"To enlarge their territory" is to extend their reputations. "They have ripped open pregnant women in Gilead in order to enlarge their territory" because heretics slay the souls of the faithful, who have already conceived in their minds some understanding of the truth, by their false preaching, and they extend their reputation for knowledge. They rend the hearts of the little ones, already pregnant from conceiving the word, with the sword of error, and make a reputation for themselves, as if for their teaching. As we try to teach these people not to think wrong thoughts we must first counsel them not to seek vainglory. When we deprive them of their root, which is pride, then the branches—that is, false assertions—wither.

We must also counsel them not to turn God's law, which was given us to prohibit sacrifice to Satan, into a sacrifice they are offering to Satan by generating errors and disagreements. The Lord complains through the prophet, "I gave her the grain, the wine and the oil, and lavished upon her silver and gold that they used for Baal." We receive grain from the Lord when, with the outer covering of the letter removed, we perceive in the kernel of the spirit the inner meaning of the law with regard to more obscure texts.[2] The Lord gives us his wine when he makes us drunk with a profound proclamation of his Scripture. He bestows his oil on us when he gently and smoothly puts order into our lives by his plainer precepts. He lavishes silver on us when he provides us with texts radiant with truth, and he enriches us

---

2. Hos. 2:8; 2 Cor. 3:6.

with gold when he illumines our hearts with an understanding of the supreme splendor.

Heretics offer all these to Baal because by their corrupt understanding of everything they lead astray the hearts of those who listen to them. Of God's grain, wine and oil, silver and gold, they make a sacrifice to Satan because they divert words of peace toward error and discord. Hence we must counsel them to consider carefully that when they perversely use the precepts of peace to bring about discord, by God's just judgment they themselves find death in the words of life.

On the other hand, we must counsel those who interpret the words of the law correctly, but who speak without humility, to examine themselves in the divine words before bringing them to others. Otherwise, when they criticize the actions of others they may abandon themselves, and while their thoughts about everything in sacred Scripture are correct, they may fail to notice one thing only, its criticism of the proud. Doctors who want to heal others while they are unaware of their own wounds are dishonest and incompetent.

Those, then, who do not speak the words of God with humility we must certainly counsel to first take note of the poison with which they are themselves infected, and only then to apply remedies to the sick; otherwise, even as they are dosing others, they themselves may die. We must counsel them to consider that their way of speaking is to be in keeping with the value of what they are saying, and that they should not preach one thing by their words and something else by their example.

These people must listen to Scripture: "Whoever speaks must do so as one speaking the words of God." Why do people presenting words not theirs swell with pride as if these words were their own? Let them listen to Scripture: "As from God, and in God's presence, we speak in Christ." Those who grasp that they have received from God the word they preach, and who seek by it to satisfy God and not other humans, speak "from God and in God's presence." Let them hear that "the arrogant are an abomination to the Lord."[3] Those who seek their own renown through God's word violate its giver's rights; they feel no anxiety about preferring their own praise to the one from whom they received the very thing being praised.

Let them hear what Solomon says to preachers: "Drink water from your own cistern, flowing water from your own well. Let your springs overflow outside, and divide the waters in the streets. Let them be for yourself alone, and not for sharing with strangers."[4]

Preachers drink from their own cisterns when they return to their hearts and are the first to listen to what they are saying. They drink flowing water from their own wells if their own words wash over them and refresh them. "Let your springs overflow outside, and divide the waters in the streets." They are right to drink first, and then flow out over others by their preaching—for springs to overflow outside is for the power of preaching to wash over others in an external way, and to divide the waters in the streets is to make the divine communication available to a great multitude of listeners in accordance with each one's character.

And because a desire for vainglory often creeps in when we bring God's word to the attention of many, after saying "divide the waters in the streets" he is right to add, "let them be for yourself alone, and not for sharing with strangers." By "strangers" he means the evil spirits, those of whom the prophet says in the words of a person being tempted, "Strangers have risen against me, the ruthless have sought my life."[5] He tells us, "Divide the waters in the streets, and let them be for yourself alone." He means, "You must serve in the world by your preaching, but do it in such

---

3. 1 Pet. 4:11; 2 Cor. 2:17; Prov. 16:5.
4. Prov. 5:15–17.
5. Ps. 54:3.

a way as not to ally yourself to unclean spirits by your pride. You are not to make your enemies your partners in the service of the divine word." We divide the waters in the streets, then, and yet keep them for ourselves, when we spread our preaching far and wide without the least intention of winning human renown in that way.

25

Preachers

W E MUST COUNSEL DIFFERENTLY those capable of preaching worthily but whom excessive humility holds back, and those debarred from it by immaturity or age, but who push heedlessly on. We must counsel those who can preach with good results, but who avoid it from exaggerated humility, to grasp from a consideration of something of less importance how much they are failing in a more important matter. If they were to hide money in their possession from their needy neighbors, beyond any doubt they would be helping them on to disaster. Let them, then, reflect on the guilt that binds them when, by withholding the words of their preaching from their sinning brothers and sisters, they are concealing the medicine of life from people who are dying. A sage put this well: "Hidden wisdom and unseen treasure, of what value is either?"[1]

If a famine was wasting people, and they kept their wheat concealed, beyond any doubt they would be a cause of death. Let them consider how those people will be punished who fail to minister the bread of grace they have received while souls are perishing from famine of the word. So Solomon says, "The people curse those who hoard grain."[2] To hoard grain is to hold back within oneself the

---

1. Sirach 20:30.
2. Prov. 11:26.

words of holy preaching. Those who do this are cursed by the people because, on account of the punishment of the many they could have set right, they are condemned solely for the fault of keeping silent.

If those not unacquainted with the art of medicine were to see a wound needing to be lanced, and yet decline to lance it, surely they would make themselves guilty of a brother's or sister's death solely by omitting to act. Let those who perceive spiritual wounds and neglect to heal them with the lance of their words see how great a fault they are involved in. The prophet says, "A curse on all who withhold their swords from bloodshed." To withhold the sword from bloodshed is to prevent the word of preaching from slaying carnal life. Scripture says of this sword that "my sword shall devour flesh."[3]

When they are concealing the word of preaching within themselves let them listen with terror to the divine judgment against themselves in order that fear may chase fear out of their hearts. Let them hear how the one who would not expend the talent lost it, with a judgment of condemnation added on. Let them hear that Paul believed himself innocent of his neighbors' blood since he did not spare himself from upbraiding them for their vices: "I swear to you this day that I am innocent of the blood of all of you, for I did not shrink from declaring to you the whole of God's purpose." Let them hear how John is counseled by an angelic voice that says, "Let everyone who hears say, 'Come!'" This is so that those to whom an inner voice finds its way may raise their own voices and draw others to the place where they themselves are being transported; if they approach the one calling them empty-handed, even they, who have been called, may find the doors closed. Let them hear how Isaiah reproaches himself with a loud cry of repentance because he refrained from serving the word after being illumined by a heavenly light: "Woe is me that I have been silent!"[4]

---

3. Jer. 48:10; Deut. 32:42.
4. Matt. 25:14–30; Acts 20:26–27; Rev. 22:17; Isa. 6:5 Vulgate.

Let them hear from Solomon the promise of a great increase in the knowledge of preaching for those not held back by the vice of torpor with respect to what they have already obtained: "Those who confer blessing will be amply enriched, those who inebriate others will themselves be inebriated." Those who confer blessing by the external activity of preaching are amply enriched interiorly, and those who do not cease from making their hearers drunk on the wine of eloquence grow increasingly drunk themselves from the cup of a vastly increased gift. Let them hear how David offered his not withholding the grace of preaching he had received as a gift to God: "See, I will not hold my tongue, as you know, O Lord; I have not hidden your righteousness within my heart; I have declared your truth and your salvation."[5]

Let them hear what the bridegroom says in conversation with his bride: "O you who dwell in the gardens, my friends are listening—let me hear your voice!"[6] The church dwells in the gardens, keeping the young plantings of virtue well tended and in a state of inner greenness. Her friends who listen for her voice are the chosen ones who long to hear the words she preaches. This voice the bridegroom longs to hear because in his chosen ones he is full of desire for her preaching.

Let them hear how Moses, seeing God angered against the people, and ordering swords taken up for vengeance, declared those to be on God's side who would unhesitatingly punish the crimes of the guilty: "If any are on the Lord's side, let them join me! Let every one put his sword on his thigh. Go back and forth from gate to gate through the middle of the camp, and let each one kill his brother, his friend, and his neighbor!"[7] To put the sword on the thigh is to set zeal for preaching before pleasures of the flesh, and so those eager to speak holy words must take care to overcome

---

5. Prov. 11:25; Ps. 40:9–10.

6. Song of Sol. 8:13.

7. Exod. 32:26–27.

every illicit suggestion that comes to their minds. To go from gate to gate is to go from vice to vice—everything by which death enters the soul—censuring all of them. To go through the middle of the camp is to live with such impartiality within the church as to convict the guilty of their faults while not turning aside with special favor for anyone.

Hence Scripture adds, "Let each one kill his brother, his friend, and his neighbor!" People kill brothers, friends, and neighbors, if they find anything punishable, when they do not spare from the sword of their rebuke even those they love because of some relationship with them. If those who are stirred up by the eagerness of divine love to castigate vices are said to be on God's side, surely those who refuse to castigate the lives of carnal persons as much as they should are denying that they are on God's side.

On the other hand, we must counsel those debarred by immaturity or age from the office of preacher, but who push heedlessly on, not to arrogate to themselves the burden of so great an office rashly, and so cut themselves off from the path to future betterment. When they undertake at the wrong time what they are incapable of doing, they lose even what they would have been able to do at the right time. They display their loss of the very knowledge that they are trying unsuitably to display.

We must counsel them to consider that if young birds want to fly before their wings are mature, their desire for the heights plunges them into the depths. We must counsel them to consider that if heavy beams are placed on a structure recently built but not yet firmly fastened together, the result is not a dwelling but a ruin. We must counsel them to consider that when women bring forth the children they have conceived before they are fully formed, they are not filling a home but a tomb.

Truth himself could in a moment have strengthened those he willed to strengthen, but to give an example to those who follow that they should not presume to preach while immature, he added after fully instructing his disciples about the power of preaching, "Stay here in the city until you are clothed with power from on high."[8] We stay in the city if we confine ourselves within the enclosure of our own selves, not roaming outside talking; when we are perfectly clothed with divine power, that is the time for us to go, as it were, outside ourselves, instructing others.

A certain sage says, "Speak scarcely, you who are young, in your own cause, and if you are questioned twice, then begin to respond."[9] Our Redeemer, who is the creator of the angels in heaven and their constant teacher, by revelation of his power, did not choose to become a teacher of human beings on earth before his thirtieth year. This was to instill in the heedless a wholesome fear, since he himself, who could not err, preached the gift of a mature life only at a mature age.

Scripture says that "when he was twelve years old, the boy Jesus stayed behind in Jerusalem," and later, when he was sought by his parents, "they found him in the temple, sitting among the teachers, listening to them and asking them questions."[10] We must pay careful attention to this. When Jesus at twelve years is described as sitting among teachers, he is found not teaching but asking questions. This example reveals that the weak should not venture to teach when Jesus, as a boy, chose to be taught by asking questions—Jesus who ministered the word of knowledge to his own teachers by the power of his divinity.

When Paul tells his disciple, "Command and teach these things. Let no one despise your youth," we should be aware that in holy Scripture young adulthood is sometimes called youth. This becomes clear if we cite Solomon: "Rejoice young man, in your youth."[11] He would not have addressed in his youth the one he calls "young man" if they were not the same thing.

---

8. Luke 24:49.
9. Sirach 32:7–8.
10. Luke 2:42–43, 46.
11. 1 Tim. 4:11–12; Eccl. 11:9.

26

Successes and Failures

W E MUST COUNSEL DIFFERENTLY those successful in fulfilling their temporal desires, and those who, though they crave what is of the world, are worn out by toil and adversity. We must counsel those successful in fulfilling their temporal desires that when everything corresponds to what they want, they should not neglect to seek the giver while their hearts are bound to what is given. They should not care more for the journey than for their homeland, or turn their provisions for the trip into obstacles to their arrival, or refuse to look at the brightness of the sun because of their pleasure in moonlight at night.

We must counsel them to regard whatever they attain in this world as consolation in calamity, not as reward or recompense; they must stiffen their resistance to the world's favors so as not to succumb to them through their whole-hearted delight in them. Those who do not put down, in their heart's judgment, any success they may experience because of their love of a better life, convert this passing life's favor into an occasion for everlasting death. Those who rejoice over their worldly successes are rebuked in the person of the people of Edom, who allowed themselves to be overcome by their own prosperity: "They took possession of my land as their inheritance, with joy, and with their whole heart and mind."[1] We see by these words that they

---

1. Ezek. 36:5.

were severely chastised not simply because they rejoiced, but because they rejoiced "with their whole heart and mind."

Solomon says, "The waywardness of the simple will kill them, and the success of fools will destroy them," and Paul counsels, "Let those who buy be as though they had no possessions, and those who deal with the world as though they had no dealings with it."[2] This means that what is put at our disposal should serve us outwardly in such a way as not to turn us from pursuing the pleasures of heaven, and the things offered us as aids in our exile should not reduce the distress of our inner pilgrimage. We are not to rejoice in what is passing as if we believe ourselves happy—we who see ourselves wretched for a time in the absence of what is eternal.

The church says, in the words of those who have been chosen, "His left hand is under my head, and his right arm will embrace me."[3] She has put God's left hand—that is, success in this present life—under her head, so to speak, resting on it with perfect love. God's right arm embraces her because her complete devotion enfolds her within his eternal happiness.

Solomon, again, says, "Length of days is in her right hand, and in her left hand are riches and honor." He has taught us how we are to possess riches and honor when he notes that they are in her left hand. So the psalmist says, "Save me with your right hand"—not just with your hand, but "with your right hand"—to indicate by "right hand" that he was seeking eternal salvation. So, again, Scripture says, "Your right hand, O Lord, shattered the enemies."[4] God's enemies, though they are successful in his left hand, are broken by his right hand, since this present life ordinarily uplifts the wicked, but the coming of eternal happiness condemns them.

---

2. Prov. 1:32; 1 Cor. 7:30–31.
3. Song of Sol. 2:6.
4. Prov. 3:16; Ps. 108:6; Exod. 15:6.

We must counsel those who prosper in this world that they should be shrewd enough to consider that they are sometimes given success in this present life to stir them up to do better, and sometimes to condemn them more fully in eternal life. The land of Canaan was promised to the Israelite people to rouse them to hope some day for what is eternal.[5] That rude nation would not have trusted in God's promise for the remote future if they had not received something close at hand from the one who made the promise. Therefore to more surely strengthen their faith in what is eternal, they were drawn not only by hope to the reality, but also by the reality to hope. The psalmist clearly testifies to this: "He gave them the lands of the nations, and they took possession of the work of the people, in order that they might keep his statutes and seek out his law."[6]

When humans do not respond to God the giver with good works, they are the more justly condemned, as we believe them to have been more lovingly supported. So, again, the psalmist says, "As they were being lifted up, you cast them down." When the reprobate do not requite God's bounty with good deeds, when here below they give up entirely and abandon themselves to the successes that flow in upon them, their exterior progress brings an interior fall. The rich man being tormented in hell was told, "During your lifetime you received good things."[7] Even as a bad man he received good here on earth in order that there he could receive bad in fuller measure—here not even good had caused him to change his ways.

On the other hand, we must counsel those who, though they crave what is of the world, are worn out by toil and adversity, to give careful consideration to the fact that the creator and administrator of all things is watching over them with great love when he does not abandon them to

---

5. Exod. 3:8; Deut. 1:25; 8:7–10.
6. Ps. 105:44–45.
7. Ps. 73:18; Luke 16:25.

their own desires. When doctors lose hope, they allow their patients to take whatever they choose, while they forbid much they would like to those they believe they can cure. We take money away from the children for whom, as they are our heirs, we are maintaining an entire estate. Those humbled by adversity in the course of their temporal life must find joy in their hope of an eternal inheritance, since divine providence would not restrain those who are to be taught by the rule of discipline unless they were seen as people to be saved forever.

We must then counsel those worn out by toil and adversity in their time-bound cravings to consider carefully that the righteous are frequently caught by sin, as if by a trap, when uplifted on temporal authority. David, God's beloved, was more upright while he was a servant than after he had come into a kingdom. As a servant, he feared out of his love of righteousness to strike his enemy Saul when he was at his mercy; as king, he used a ruse to deprive a loyal soldier of life out of an impulse of lust.[8] Who, then, can seek riches, authority, or honor without blame, if blame falls on one who possessed them without having sought them? Who will be saved amidst these things without toil and great determination if one who had been prepared for them by God's choice was overwhelmed by them when sin intervened?

We must counsel these people to consider that Solomon is said to have fallen into idolatry after having been so wise.[9] No adversity in this world is recorded of him before he fell, but the wisdom granted him deserted his heart entirely because it was unguarded by any training in tribulation.

---

8. 1 Samuel 24; 2 Samuel 11.
9. 1 Kings 11.

27

The Married and the Single

WE MUST COUNSEL those bound by marriage, and those free of its ties, differently. We must counsel those bound by marriage that, while each is taking thought for the interests of the other, they should be eager to please one another without displeasing their maker. They should so act in affairs of this world as not to omit to desire the things that are God's; they should so rejoice in their present blessings as earnestly to fear eternal evils; and they should so grieve over temporal evils as to fix their hope with every encouragement on everlasting good. Thus, as they are aware that everything they do is transitory, and that what they desire is permanent, the evils of the world will not break their hearts, which are fortified by hope of heaven's blessings. While the imagined evils of the coming judgment are causing them sorrow, they will not be deceived by the blessings of this present life.

Christian spouses are both weak and steadfast. They are incapable of fully despising things temporal, and yet capable of uniting themselves by desire to things eternal. Although for the time being they exist on the plane of physical pleasure, they grow strong by being refreshed by heavenly hope. If they possess what belongs to the world for use on their journey, they must hope for what belongs to God to enjoy at their goal. They should not be so totally engaged in their present occupations as to turn entirely away from what they ought firmly to hope for.

Paul expresses this briefly and well: "Let those who have spouses be as though they had none, and those who mourn as though they were not mourning, and those who rejoice as though they were not rejoicing."[1] People have spouses as though having none when their enjoyment of physical pleasure with their spouses never turns them, as a result of their mutual love, toward wrongdoing, and away from a straightforward purpose of improvement. They have spouses as though having none when they see that everything is transitory, and endure the concerns of their flesh out of necessity while waiting, out of desire, for the everlasting joys of the spirit. To mourn without mourning is to lament over outward misfortune while knowing how to rejoice in the consolation of eternal hope. To rejoice without rejoicing is to take heart from what is below while never losing one's awe of what is supreme.

Paul almost immediately adds, "for the form of this world is passing away."[2] He means, "Do not have a constant love for the world because the world you love cannot be constant. For you to attach your hearts there, as if you were staying on, is futile, when the world you love is detaching itself."

We must counsel spouses to bear patiently whatever either one does that displeases the other, and to save one another by their prayers. Scripture says, "Bear one another's burdens, and in this way you will fulfill the law of Christ."[3] Christ's law is love. For love he has conferred his blessings on us in abundance, and borne our evils in patience. We fulfill the law of Christ by imitating him when we too confer our blessings liberally, and lovingly put up with the wrongs done by our fellow human beings. We must also counsel them to keep in mind not so much what each endures from

---

1. 1 Cor. 7:29–30.
2. 1 Cor. 7:31.
3. Gal. 6:2.

the other, as what the other has to endure. If they consider what the other must put up with in them, they bear more lightly what they put up with in the other.

We must counsel spouses that they have been united for the purpose of producing offspring. When they give themselves to immoderate intercourse they turn the means of procreation to the service of sensuality. They should reflect that although they are not then going outside the rights of marriage, they are exceeding those rights within the marriage. For this reason they must efface by frequent prayers what they disfigure by mingling it with sensuality—the beauty of intercourse itself.

The apostle Paul was skilled in heavenly medicine. Less to instruct the strong than to provide a remedy for the weak, he said, "Concerning the matters about which you wrote, it is good for a man not to touch a woman. But because of cases of sexual immorality, each man should have his own wife and each woman her own husband." As he first mentioned his anxiety about sexual immorality, clearly he was not giving a commandment for those who were standing but indicating a bench to those who were falling, to prevent them from collapsing on the ground. Still addressing the weak he added, "The husband should give to his wife her conjugal rights, and likewise the wife to her husband." To those for whom he was granting a measure of sensuality in the noble estate of marriage he adds, "This I say by way of concession, not of command."[4] When he speaks of concession he implies that a fault is present, a fault he quickly exonerates. He does this because the fault is not in the act, which is lawful, but in not keeping the lawful act under control.

We see this represented in Lot.[5] Lot fled from Sodom as it was burning, but on reaching Zoar he put off his ascent of the mountains. To flee Sodom as it is burning is to turn

---

4. 1 Cor. 7:1, 3, 6.
5. Genesis 19.

away from the unlawful fires of the flesh; the mountain height is the purity of those who are physically chaste. Those who engage in sexual intercourse, but do not indulge in sensuality beyond what is necessary for producing offspring, are surely like people on a mountain. To stand on the mountain is to seek from the flesh only the joy of having descendants. To stand on the mountain is to hold fast to the flesh in a nonfleshly way.

But since many repudiate the gross faults of the flesh without limiting themselves only to their conjugal rights within marriage, Lot leaves Sodom but does not immediately reach the mountains. These people immediately abandon a reprehensible life, but are not yet really on the peak of married continence. Midway is the city of Zoar, where a weak person in flight can find refuge. When spouses come together without restraint, they avoid gross faults, and are saved by mercy. They find, as it were, a little city; there they can be protected from the fires, because such a married life, while not a marvel of the virtues, is still secure from punishment.

Lot says to the angel, "That city is near enough to flee to, and it is a little one; I will be safe in it. Is it not a little one? I will live in it." The city is described as near, and yet as out of danger—married life is neither separated and at a distance from the world, nor is it foreign to the joy of salvation. Spouses preserve their lives as if in a little city only when they intercede for each other with constant prayer. Hence the angel rightly said to Lot, "See, in this too I have received your prayer; I will not overthrow the city of which you have spoken." When prayer is poured out to God, the life of such a couple is not condemned. Paul too gives us advice concerning such prayer: "Do not deprive one another except perhaps by agreement for a set time, to devote yourselves to prayer."[6]

On the other hand, we must counsel those not bound by marriage that they are to observe the heavenly precepts

---

6. 1 Cor. 7:5.

more strictly in that the yoke of physical union does not incline them toward worldly concerns. Since they are not weighed down by the lawful burden of marriage, they should not be oppressed by an unlawful load of earthly anxiety. The less encumbered they are, the more ready should the last day find them; if they neglect to do the good for which they have the leisure, they will deserve worse punishment.

Let them listen to what Paul says when instructing certain people on the gift of celibacy, not rejecting marriage, but only the worldly cares that spring from it: "I say this for your own benefit, not to put a restraint on you, but to promote good order and unhindered devotion to the Lord."[7] Marriage produces earthly anxieties, and the teacher of the nations is urging his listeners on to better things so that they will not be involved with them. When the unmarried are hindered by secular concerns, they are not subject to marriage, but neither have they escaped its burdens.

We must counsel the unmarried not to suppose that they can have sexual intercourse with other unmarried persons without a judgment of condemnation. When Paul includes the vice of fornication among the many detestable offenses, he is indicating its guilty nature: "No fornicators, idolaters, adulterers, degenerates, male prostitutes, thieves, misers, drunkards, slanderers, or swindlers will possess the kingdom of God," and again, "God will judge fornicators and adulterers."[8]

We must counsel them that if they are enduring storms of temptation, with risk to their salvation, they are to seek the harbor of marriage. Scripture says, "It is better to marry than to be on fire." They come blamelessly to marriage if they have not yet vowed anything better. Those who have resolved on a greater good make a lesser one, although lawful, unlawful. Scripture says, "No one who puts a hand to

---

7. 1 Cor. 7:35.
8. 1 Cor. 6:9; Heb. 13:4.

the plow and looks back is fit for the kingdom of heaven."[9] Those who have set a more courageous goal before them are plainly convicted of looking back if they relinquish the greater good and return to the lesser.

9. 1 Cor. 7:9; Luke 9:62.

28

The Chaste and the Unchaste

WE MUST COUNSEL those aware of sins of the flesh and those unfamiliar with them differently. We must counsel those who have experienced the sins of the flesh that after a shipwreck they should at least have a fear of the sea, and a horror of the familiar dangers where they can be lost. Otherwise those mercifully preserved after doing wrong may die by shamelessly repeating the wrong. Scripture tells those who sin and do not cease, "You have the forehead of a whore; you have refused to be ashamed."[1]

We must then counsel them to see to it that, if they have chosen not to preserve their natural goodness in its integrity, at least they mend it when they have torn it. They must consider how many in the great body of believers keep themselves pure, and turn others back from error as well. What will they say if, while others retain their integrity, they do not come to their senses even after doing harm to themselves? What will they say if, when many bring others along with them into the kingdom, they do not bring even themselves back to the Lord, who is awaiting them?

We must counsel them to consider their past sins and to avoid those that threaten them. Through the prophet the Lord recalls their past faults to the memories of those corrupted in this world, as represented by Judah, so that they may be ashamed to dishonor themselves in the future:

---

1. Jer. 3:3.

"They played the whore in Egypt; they played the whore in their youth; their breasts were caressed there, and their virgin bosoms were bruised."[2] Breasts are caressed in Egypt when humans surrender their wills to the depraved desires of this world; virgin bosoms are bruised in Egypt when the natural senses, which still possess their integrity, are corrupted by the impulses of lust.

We must counsel those who have experienced the sins of the flesh to observe with special care the great benevolence with which God opens his heart to us when we return to him after transgressing. He says through the prophet, "If a man divorces his wife, and she leaves him and marries another man, will he return to her again? Will not that woman be dishonored and defiled? You have prostituted yourself with many lovers: yet return to me, says the Lord."[3] Notice how the argument concerning a woman who prostitutes herself and is abandoned is based on justice, and yet God shows us faithful love and not justice when we return to him after a fall. We are surely meant to infer from this that if we are pardoned with such love when we transgress, how shamelessly we sin when we do not return after transgressing! What pardon will there be for the wicked from the one who, after their fault, does not cease to call?

The compassion expressed in a call after a transgression is well stated by the prophet when he says to one who has turned away, "Your eyes shall see your teacher, and your ears shall hear the word of one counseling you behind your back."[4] The Lord counseled the human race to their face when he disclosed what they should do and not do to the humans created in Paradise and in possession of free will. The humans turned their back to God's face when they flouted his commandments out of pride. Yet God did not abandon them in their pride; he gave the law to call them

---

2. Ezek. 23:3.
3. Jer. 3:1.
4. Isa. 30:20–21.

back, he sent angels who offered encouragement, he appeared in our mortal flesh. Therefore God, who called us to recover his grace even after we had spurned him, stood behind our back to counsel us.

What can be said generally of everyone must be understood of each in particular. As if standing in God's presence, each of us perceives the words of God's counsel when we recognize the precepts of his will before we commit sin. To remain standing before God's face is not yet to spurn him by sinning. When we forsake our innocence, and desire and choose wickedness, we turn our backs to God's face. But look—even behind our backs God follows us and counsels us; even after our faults he urges us to return to him. He calls back those who have turned away, he has no regard for what they have done, he opens his heart to those who turn back. We hear the voice of one counseling us behind our backs if, after our sins, we at least turn back to the Lord who is inviting us. We ought, then, to be ashamed on account of the loving-kindness of the one calling us even if we choose not to fear his justice. Our wickedness in spurning him is greater in that he does not refuse to continue calling us even when we have spurned him.

On the other hand, we must counsel those ignorant of sins of the flesh that the taller they stand the more they have to fear falling headlong. We must counsel them that the more prominent is the place on which they stand, the more frequent are the attacks of the one lying in ambush for them. His energy in rousing himself equals the firmness with which he sees himself withstood; his inability to tolerate being withstood is greater as he sees an unbroken battle line of frail flesh opposed to himself. We must counsel them to keep their reward continually in mind, and then without any doubt they will gladly scorn the hardships of the temptations they put up with. If their eyes are fixed on the happiness that does not pass away when once attained, their passing troubles become light.

Let them listen to the prophet: "Thus says the Lord to the eunuchs: To those who keep my sabbath, who choose the things that please me, and who hold fast my covenant, I will give, in my house and within my walls, a place and a name better than sons and daughters." Eunuchs are those who cut off wrongdoing in themselves by restraining the impulses of the flesh. We see their place with the Father—in the Father's house, that is, in their eternal home, they are even placed ahead of the children! Let them listen to John: "These are the ones who have not defiled themselves with women; they are virgins, who follow the Lamb wherever he goes." They sing "a song that no one can utter except the one hundred forty-four thousand."[5] To sing the song of the Lamb as a celibate is to rejoice with him forever, at the head of all the faithful, even with incorrupt flesh. The rest of the chosen are able to hear this song, although they cannot utter it; even though they have not risen to the reward of those who sing it, love makes them rejoice in their high state.

Those unfamiliar with sins of the flesh should hear what Truth himself says of this state of integrity: "Not everyone can accept this teaching."[6] In denying that it belongs to everyone he is asserting that it is supreme. In foretelling that it will be difficult to accept, he is teaching his hearers that once begun they must take every precaution to preserve it.

We must counsel those with no experience of sins of the flesh to remain aware that virginity is more excellent than marriage while not thinking themselves superior to those who are married. Then, as they put virginity in the first place, and themselves last, they may better preserve what they esteem even as they guard against vain self-exaltation.

We must counsel them to consider that the conduct of people of the world is often a reproach to the lives of the continent when the former do works beyond what is required, and the latter do not rouse their hearts to accord

---

5. Isa. 56:4–5; Rev. 14:4, 3.
6. Matt. 19:11.

with their way of life. So the prophet says, "Be ashamed, Sidon, says the sea."[7] Sidon is brought to shame by the voice of the sea, so to speak, when the lives of those who are protected, and supposedly steadfast, are condemned by comparison with the lives of the worldly, who are being tossed about in this world.

People who return to the Lord after committing sins of the flesh often show themselves more energetic in doing good the more they see themselves liable to condemnation because of the bad they have done. Often too, when those who remain physically pure see that they have nothing to weep for, they reckon that the innocence of their lives is enough, and do nothing to rouse themselves to spiritual fervor.

A life burning with love after a fault is ordinarily more pleasing to God than innocence become torpid from a sense of security. Hence the words of our judge: "Her many sins will be forgiven her because she has loved much," and, "There will be more joy in heaven over one person who repents than over ninety-nine righteous persons who need no repentance."[8] We can readily gather this from our own experience if we consider our own judgments. We have more love for land that produces a rich harvest after being cleared of thorns than for land that never had thorns, but that produces only a meager crop when we cultivate it.

We must counsel those with no experience of sins of the flesh not to put themselves ahead of others because of their superior state when they are ignorant of how many better things those inferior to them may be doing. At our examination by the righteous judge, the value of our actions alters what our state of life has earned. In the realm of appearances, who does not know that among gems the carbuncle is preferred to the jacinth?—and yet people prefer a sky blue jacinth to a pale carbuncle. The beauty in one supplies

---

7. Isa. 23:4.
8. Luke 7:47; 15:7.

what nature does not provide, while the poor quality of its color spoils the other, which nature has set before it. Among humans, some who are in a better state of life are worse, and some in a worse state of life are better, because the latter transcend their lower condition by living good lives, while the former fall short of their superior place by failing to live up to it.

29

Sinners in Deed and in Thought

WE MUST COUNSEL DIFFERENTLY those who grieve over their sinful actions and those who grieve over their sinful thoughts. We must counsel those who grieve over their sinful actions that perfect sorrow washes away the wrongs they have done. Then what they owe for what they have done will not bind them more tightly, but be satisfied by their tears of reparation. Scripture says, "You have given us tears to drink in full measure."[1] Each of us should drink tears of compunction in repentance as we recall the measure that our faults have dried us up, away from God.

We must counsel them to recall what they have done continually before their eyes; by looking at these things themselves they may contrive that their strict judge does not have to look at them. Hence before David asked, "Turn your eyes away from my sins," he said, "My sin is always before me." He means, "I ask you not to regard my sin because I am always regarding it." The Lord says through the prophet, "I will not remember your sins, but do you remember them."[2]

We must counsel them to consider their sins one by one. Then, as they grieve over the stain produced by each mistake they may at once cleanse themselves completely by

---

1. Ps. 80:5.
2. Ps. 51:9, 3; Isa. 43:25, after the Septuagint.

their tears. Jeremiah says, when weighing each of Judah's transgressions, "My eyes flow with streams of water."[3] Our eyes shed streams of water when our tears flow separately over each sin. Our minds do not grieve over all of them equally at one and the same time, but when the memory, now of one, now of another, touches us more sharply, we are cleansed from all together by the emotion each brings forth.

We must counsel them to count on the mercy they are asking for so that they will not perish by violent and immoderate regret. The Lord in his loving-kindness would not have put before transgressors' eyes the sins they are to weep for if he had wanted to punish them severely by himself. Clearly he whose mercy comes before everything we do has chosen to hide from his judgment those he has made their own judges. Scripture says, "Let us come before him in confession," and Paul says, "If we judged ourselves, we would not be judged."[4]

Again, we must counsel them to trust in their hope in such a way as not to grow listless out of an inconsiderate feeling of security. When our cunning enemy sees people he has overthrown by sin troubled over their fall, he frequently uses soft words to seduce them into a dangerous sense of security. We see this figuratively when we recall what was done to Dinah: "Dinah went out to visit the women of that land. When Shechem, son of Hamor the Hivite, chief of that land, saw her, he loved her deeply, seized her and slept with her, overwhelming the virgin by force. His soul was bound to her, and he spoke tenderly to her in her grief."[5] Dinah goes out to visit the women of a strange land when we neglect our own duties, and wander outside our own condition and state of life, concerning ourselves with what others are doing. Shechem, chief of the land, overwhelms us, because the devil corrupts those found preoccupied with external affairs.

---

3. Lam. 3:48.
4. Ps. 95:2; 1 Cor. 11:31.
5. Gen. 34:1–3.

"His soul was bound to her" because he saw it united to himself by evil. When we recover after a fault, we feel condemned; we try to weep for what we have done, but the corrupter calls empty hopes and assurances before our eyes so as to take from us all the benefits of our grief. Rightly then does Scripture add that "he spoke tenderly to her in her grief." At one time he tells us of worse things done by others, at another time he assures us that what we did was nothing; he says at one time that God is compassionate, and at still another he promises us time to repent. He wants us to fall into his trap and suspend our purpose of repentance. Thus, as no evils now cause us grief, we will receive nothing good hereafter; and as now we even enjoy our transgressions, then we will be more thoroughly overwhelmed with punishment.

On the other hand, we must counsel those who weep over their sinful thoughts to consider carefully, deep in their hearts, whether they have transgressed only by the pleasure they felt, or by consent as well. Ordinarily when a heart is tempted it feels pleasure owing to the sinfulness of the flesh, and yet struggles by its reason against this sinfulness; thus in its inmost thought what pleases makes it sad, and what makes it sad pleases. Sometimes, however, the spirit is so engulfed by temptation that it puts up no struggle at all, but deliberately pursues the pleasure that strikes it. If an exterior opportunity offered itself, it would soon fulfill its interior desire. To our strict judge's righteous gaze this is no longer a guilty thought; it is a guilty action, because although the difficulties of the situation have put off the sin outside, the will has committed it inside by its act of consent.

We have learned from the case of our first parents that we commit the evil of every fault in three stages: suggestion, pleasure, and consent. The first is brought about by the enemy, the second by our flesh, the third by our spirit. The one who sets snares for us suggests something wrong, the flesh gives in to the pleasure, and at last the spirit, being overcome by the pleasure, consents. In the case mentioned, the serpent suggested something wrong, Eve (whom we may take to be the flesh) gave herself up to the pleasure, and Adam (the spirit), overcome by the suggestion and the pleasure, gave his consent. We come to know sin by suggestion, we are vanquished by pleasure, and we are bound by consent.

We must then counsel those who weep over the depravity of their thoughts to consider carefully how far into sin they have fallen so as to raise in themselves a degree of sorrow proportionate to their fall, as they feel it within themselves. If they fail to grieve over their evil thoughts these may lead them to carry out the actions. But the fear these things should inspire must not dishearten them. The merciful God often washes away the sins of the heart more quickly by not allowing them to issue in actions, and our wrong thoughts are absolved more readily because we are not strictly bound by the effects of the act. So the psalmist rightly says, "I said, 'I will confess against myself my transgressions to the Lord,' and you forgave the impiety of my heart."[6] By saying "impiety of my heart" he indicated that he wanted to confess his transgressions of thought, and when he says, "I have said, 'I will confess,'" he immediately adds "and you have forgiven," showing how easily they are pardoned. While he was still promising to ask he obtained what he was promising to ask for! Since his sin had not come to the act, his repentance would not reach the point of punishment. An afflicting thought could cleanse his heart because only an evil thought had defiled it.

---

6. Ps. 32:5.

30

The Repentant and the Unrepentant

WE MUST COUNSEL DIFFERENTLY those who weep for what they have done but do not stop doing it, and those who stop sinning but do not weep. We must counsel those who weep for what they have done but do not stop doing it to consider carefully and realize that their tears do not cleanse them if they continue to defile themselves by living wretchedly. They are only bathing themselves with their tears in order to return, once they are clean, into the dirt. Scripture speaks of a "dog returned to its vomit, and a sow that was washed, to her wallowing in the mire."[1]

When a dog vomits it throws up the food that oppressed its stomach, and when it returns to its vomit it burdens itself again with what it had been relieved of. By confessing it, those who weep for what they have done throw up the evil with which they were unfortunately filled and that oppressed the depths of their spirits; when they do it again after their confession, they are taking in the evil again.

When a sow bathes in her muddy wallow she becomes dirtier still. Those who weep for what they have done but do not stop doing it make themselves subject to punishment for a graver sin. Those who treat lightly the forgiveness their tears bring them roll around, so to speak, in muddy water; when they fail to unite clean living with their weeping, they make even their tears dirty in God's sight.

---

1. 2 Pet. 2:22.

Again, Scripture says, "Do not repeat a word in your prayer." To repeat a word in prayer is to commit after weeping what we have to weep for again. Therefore Isaiah tells us, "Wash yourselves, make yourselves clean!" Those who fail to maintain a blameless life after they have wept do not care about being clean after a bath. Those who do not stop weeping for what they have done, but do again what they have to weep for, are washed but are not clean. A sage says, "If someone washes after touching a corpse, and touches it again, what has been gained by the washing?"[2] Those who are cleansed by weeping after a sin are washed after touching a corpse, but those who repeat their fault after weeping touch the corpse after the washing.

We must counsel those who weep for what they have done but do not stop doing it to recognize that in the eyes of their severe judge they are like people who fawn over others obsequiously in their presence, but cruelly inflict on them all the hostility and harm they can manage when they leave them. What does weeping for a fault amount to if it does not give evidence of our humble attachment to God? And what does doing wrong after weeping amount to if not that we are behaving with arrogant hostility toward the one to whom we have prayed? James testifies to this when he says, "Whoever wishes to be a friend of the world becomes an enemy of God."[3]

We must counsel those who weep for what they have done but do not stop doing it to consider carefully that remorse does not normally produce righteousness in the wicked, just as temptation to sin does not normally produce harm in the good. Thus a wonderful conformity between inner disposition and the measure of a person's merit comes about, so that the wicked, when they do some part of a good deed without bringing it to completion, have a proud confidence even while they are carrying out evil deeds to

---

2. Sirach 7:14; Isa. 1:16; Sirach 34:30.
3. James 4:4.

the full; and the good, when tempted concerning some wicked deed to which they give no consent, direct their hearts more truly toward righteousness through humility in that they falter from weakness.

Balaam, looking out over the tents of the righteous, said, "Let me die the death of the righteous, and let my last end be like theirs!"[4] When, however, his time of remorse had passed, he offered counsel against the lives of those he had asked to resemble, even in their dying, and when he found an occasion for greed he promptly forgot the innocence he had wished for.

Paul says, "I see in my members another law at war with the law of my mind, making me captive to the law of sin that dwells in my members."[5] In fact, he is being tempted that he may be confirmed more staunchly in good from his recognition of his own weakness. Why was Balaam filled with remorse, while yet failing to approach righteousness, and Paul tempted, while yet not sullying himself with a fault, unless to show clearly that uncompleted good does not help the wicked, nor does unconsummated evil condemn the good?

On the other hand, we must counsel those who stop sinning but do not weep not to suppose that their faults are now pardoned; they are no longer repeating them, but they are not being cleansed by tears. Writers who stop writing do not obliterate what they have written by not adding to it; those who insult others do not make amends by keeping silent—they have to counter their earlier arrogant words by subsequent words of humility; debtors are not quit because they have stopped adding to their debts unless they have paid off those that bind them. So too, when we offend God, turning away from our wrongdoing does not make amends unless we follow up the pleasures we have loved with the lamentations opposed to them.

---

4. Num. 23:10.
5. Rom. 7:23.

Even if we were unsullied by any wrong actions during our lifetime, our innocence would not be enough to make us secure while we are still living here below because much that is forbidden would continue to disturb our hearts. How can those who have done wrong be sure of themselves when they bear witness against themselves that they are not innocent?

God is not gratified by our sufferings; God heals the diseases of sin by remedies that oppose them, so that we who have departed from him by delightful pleasures may return by bitter tears, and that we who fell by releasing ourselves to what is forbidden may also rise by restraining ourselves even in what is allowed. Wholesome sorrow must dry a heart flooded by foolish joy, and the lowliness of a humble life must heal what the elevation of pride has wounded. Scripture says, "I said to the wicked, 'Do not act wickedly,' and to transgressors, 'Do not lift up your horn.'" Transgressors lift up their horn if they do not lower themselves by repentance out of a recognition of their wickedness. So Scripture also says, "A broken and humble heart God does not despise."[6] Those who weep for their sins but do not stop doing them break their hearts all right, but they disdain to humble them; those who stop sinning without weeping for their sins humble themselves, but they refuse to break their hearts.

Paul says, "This is what some of you were. But you were washed, you were sanctified." A reformed life sanctifies those whom an uncomfortable washing with tears cleanses by repentance. Peter counsels those he sees terrified by reflection on their bad deeds, "Repent, and be baptized every one of you."[7] Before speaking of baptism he mentions penitential sorrow, so that they will first bathe in the water of their own affliction, and afterward wash themselves by the sacrament of baptism. How can those who neglect to

---

6. Ps. 75:4; 51:17.
7. 1 Cor. 6:11; Acts 2:38.

weep for their past faults live in certainty of pardon when the supreme pastor of the church believed that repentance had to be added to the sacrament that is our chief means of destroying sins?

31

People Conscious of Sin

WE MUST COUNSEL DIFFERENTLY those who go so far as to praise the wrong they do, and those who condemn their wrongdoing without avoiding it. We must counsel those who go so far as to praise the wrong they do to consider that they usually go further astray in their words than in their deeds. In deeds they alone do wrong, while by their words they are responsible for the evil done by as many persons as hear them teaching evil by their praise for it. We must then counsel them that if they are unwilling to eradicate wickedness they must at least be afraid of propagating it. We must counsel them to be content with their own ruin.

Again, we must counsel them that if they are not afraid of being wicked they should at least be ashamed of letting themselves seem so. Ordinarily we avoid the faults that we conceal, because when we are ashamed to seem what we are not afraid to be, eventually we are ashamed to be what we want to avoid seeming to be. When, however, wrong-doers shamelessly seek to be known as such, the more freely they commit every kind of outrage, the more do they even reckon them allowable, and beyond all doubt they plunge deeper into what they imagine is allowed.

Scripture says, "They have proclaimed their sin like Sodom, they have not hidden it." If Sodom had hidden its sin, it would still have sinned, but in fear. Sodom had completely lost the deterrent of fear, however, and did not even look for darkness to hide its fault. So Scripture also says, "How great is the outcry of Sodom and Gomorrah!"[1] Sin with a voice is a sin in action, but sin with an outcry is a deliberate fault.

On the other hand, we must counsel those who condemn their wrongdoing without avoiding it to look ahead and reflect on what they will say in their own defense at God's strict judgment; even when they judge themselves they cannot be excused for the guilt of their offenses. What are they but people who summon themselves to judgment? They bring charges against their faults, and arraign themselves by their actions.

We must counsel them to see that by the now hidden retribution of judgment they are given the light to see the evil that they commit, but do not strive to overcome it. The better they see, the worse is their ruin, because they perceive the light of understanding but do not relinquish the darkness of wrongdoing. Their neglect of the insight given to help them turns it into evidence against themselves. The light of understanding, which they have received to enable them to blot out their sins, increases their punishment. In their wickedness, as they do the evil their judgment condemns, they have a foretaste of the coming judgment. While being held liable to eternal punishment they are not meanwhile absolved here on earth by their self-examination. They will experience torments hereafter as severe as the evils that they do not abandon here even though they themselves condemn them.

Truth says, "The slave who knew what his master wanted but did not prepare himself and do what was wanted will receive a severe beating," and the psalmist says, "Let them go down alive to hell."[2] The living are aware and conscious of what is done to them, but the dead can feel nothing. They would go down dead to hell if they did evil without being aware of it. When they know evil, and yet do it, they "go down alive," wretched, and conscious, to the hell of wickedness.

---

1. Isa. 3:9; Gen. 18:20.
2. Luke 12:47; Ps. 55:15.

32

The Impulsive
and the Deliberate

W E MUST COUNSEL DIFFERENTLY those overcome by sudden desires and those who deliberately bind themselves by their faults. We must counsel
those a sudden desire overcomes to consider that every day
they are engaged in the warfare that this present life is. They
must cover their hearts, which cannot foresee when they may
be wounded, with the shield of vigilant fear. They should
dread the weapons of our enemy who is lurking nearby, and
protect themselves in their interior fortress during so uncer-
tain a struggle by remaining continually alert. A heart that
abandons its vigilant circumspection is liable to be wounded
since our cunning enemy can strike more freely at a breast he
finds uncovered by the breastplate of forethought.

We must counsel those overcome by sudden desires to
lay aside their excessive preoccupation with worldly things.
While they are involving themselves immoderately with
what is transitory they fail to perceive the missiles—faults—
that pierce them. Solomon gives us the words of a person
who is struck and who sleeps on:"They have beaten me but
I did not suffer; they dragged me along but I did not feel it.
When shall I awake and find wine again?"[1] Those sleeping,
careless of their own interests, are beaten and do not suffer;
they neither foresee the evils that menace them nor are
aware of those they have committed. They are dragged

---

1. Prov. 23:35.

along and feel nothing because, while the vices are leading them along by their allurements, nothing rouses them to guard themselves. They wish to be awake in order to find wine again because, although the torpor of sleep prevents their guarding themselves, yet they strive to be awake to the concerns of the world so as to be constantly drunk on pleasure. While they are asleep to what they have an obligation to be fully awake to, they are eager to be awake to what we might praise them for being asleep to.

Just before those last words Scripture says, "And you will be like one sleeping in the midst of the sea, and like a pilot fast asleep when the tiller is lost."[2] Those who neglect to provide for the movement of the vices that attack them like threatening billows are asleep in the midst of the sea while they are experiencing this world's temptations. The pilot loses the tiller, so to speak, when the spirit loses its concern for guiding the ship, by which is meant the body. To lose the tiller in the sea is to fail to concentrate on what is ahead during the violent storm of this age. A pilot holds the tiller carefully, sometimes steering the ship directly into the waves, and sometimes cutting across the force of the winds; in the same way a person's spirit, watchfully guiding the soul, rises above and cuts through some things, and foresees and avoids others, overcoming the present with effort, and with foresight gaining strength to face future conflicts.

Again, Scripture describes the valiant soldiers of our country above as having "their sword at their thigh because of alarms by night."[3] The sword is put upon the thigh when by its keenness holy preaching prevails over the perverse suggestions of the flesh. Because at night we do not see what threatens us, night represents the blindness of our weakness. They all put "their sword at their thigh because of alarms by night" since the saints, fearing what they do not see, always stand ready to take part in the struggle.

---

2. Prov. 23:34.
3. Song of Sol. 3:8.

So again, the bride is told, "Your nose is like a tower of Lebanon."[4] We often perceive by its odor what our eyes fail to see, and by our noses we discriminate between fragrance and stench. What do we mean by the church's nose, then, if not the farsighted discernment of the saints? It is likened to a tower of Lebanon because this discerning prudence is set on a height so as to see the struggles with temptation even before they arrive, and to be fortified to withstand them when they do come. What has been foreseen has less strength when it is present; when we are well prepared for a blow, the enemy, who counts on surprising us, is unnerved by the very fact of being anticipated.

On the other hand, we must counsel those who deliberately bind themselves by their faults to consider, looking to the future, that when they do evil by their own choice they are bringing a stricter judgment against themselves. Their sentence will strike them the harder as the bonds of deliberate choice confine them more tightly in their faults. They might perhaps wash away their transgressions more quickly by penitence if they fell into them only from impetuosity. A sin done by choice is more slowly undone. If people did not disdain the eternal, they would not of their own choice perish in their faults.

Those who perish deliberately differ from those who fall by impetuosity. When the former fall from a state of righteousness by sinning they often fall at the same time into the trap of despair. The Lord is not censuring wrongs done impetuously as much as our attachment to transgressing when he says through the prophet, "or else my wrath will go forth like fire and burn with no one to quench it because of the wickedness of your purposes." Again, he says in anger, "I will attend to you for the results of your purposes."[5] As sins committed deliberately differ from other sins, then, the Lord is censuring not so much the wrongs

---

4. Song of Sol. 7:4.
5. Jer. 4:4; 23:2.

done as our purpose to do wrong. In the case of actions, the sin often occurs through weakness or negligence, while an attachment to sin is always caused by a malicious intention.

The prophet well states the opposite position when he says that the blessed "did not sit on the bench of scoffers."[6] Judges and those who preside sit on benches. To "sit on the bench of scoffers" is to commit wrong deliberately; to "sit on the bench of scoffers" is to discern evil by one's reason and yet intentionally to do it. Those who are so uplifted by the arrogance of iniquity that they try to execute evil even with counsel are seated, as it were, on the bench of perverse counsel. As those supported by the dignity of the bench are superior to the crowd standing around, so sins chosen on purpose surpass the wrongs done by those who fall by impetuosity. We must then counsel those who go so far as to bind themselves in their faults with counsel to conclude what retribution will someday strike those who are now becoming not the companions of wrongdoers but their leaders!

---

6. Ps. 1:1.

33

Little Sinners and Great

W E MUST COUNSEL DIFFERENTLY those who commit small wrongs, but do them frequently, and those who keep themselves from little sins while sometimes being overwhelmed by grave ones. We must counsel those who overstep in small matters, but do this frequently, to consider not the quality but the quantity of what they do. If they scorn to be afraid when they are weighing up their actions, they ought to be alarmed when they count them. Small but numberless drops of rain fill the deep channels of the rivers. Bilgewater as it rises accomplishes imperceptibly what a rain storm does perceptibly. Small are the eruptions of scabies on the body, but when many of them cover it they bring physical life to an end as surely as does a single severe chest wound. Scripture says, "One who makes light of little things falls little by little."[1] Those who neglect to lament and avoid little sins fall completely from their righteous state, not indeed all at once, but by degrees.

We must counsel those who frequently overstep in small matters to consider carefully that sometimes little sins are worse than more serious faults. As we may recognize a serious fault more quickly, so too we may more speedily correct it; a small fault that we take to be nothing is worse in that we continue to commit it without anxiety. Hence people who have grown accustomed to slight evils are often not

---

1. Sirach 19:1.

greatly distressed by serious ones; strengthened by their faults they achieve a kind of warrant for depravity, and they despise fear in the case of more serious sins to the extent that they have learned to sin without fear in little ones.

On the other hand, we must counsel those who keep themselves from little sins while sometimes being overwhelmed by grave ones to make an effort to know themselves. While their hearts are elated over their avoidance of small sins they are swallowed up in the pit of their pride to the point of committing graver ones. Outwardly they master their little sins, but inwardly they swell up with vainglory; as on the inside they are overcome by the sickness of pride, they degrade themselves by greater evils, even outwardly.

We must then counsel those who keep themselves from little sins while sometimes being overwhelmed by grave ones not to fall interiorly while supposing that they are standing upright. If they do, by the reckoning of the strict judge their pride in their lesser righteousness would become a path leading them to the pit of greater sin. Those who in their vain pride attribute their maintenance of a small amount of goodness to their own strength are overwhelmed by graver faults when justly left to themselves; they learn by their falls that they were not standing upright on their own. In this way vast evils can restrain a heart made proud by its meager goodness.

We must counsel them to consider that in their graver faults they bind themselves deeply by guilt, yet ordinarily they sin worse in their little observances. By their grave faults they do evil, and through their little observances they hide from people that they are evil. When they do wrong in the sight of God their iniquity is evident, and when they practice a small act of goodness before people their sanctity is fraudulent.

This is why Jesus told the Pharisees, "You strain out a gnat and swallow a camel." He means that they discern trifling evils and devour greater ones. The voice of Truth is rebuking them when they are told, "You tithe mint, dill, and cumin, and leave aside the weightier matters of the law: justice, mercy, and faith."[2] We should not listen heedlessly to this, because when Jesus spoke of the tithe on little things he chose to mention the humblest herbs, which yet are sweet smelling. This was to show that when hypocrites observe little things they seek to spread the fragrance of a good opinion about themselves; although they neglect to fulfill the most important things, they observe those insignificant ones that may spread the perfume of human opinion far and wide.

---

2. Matt. 23:24, 23.

34

Nonstarters and Quitters

WE MUST COUNSEL DIFFERENTLY those who do not even begin to do good, and those who do not finish what they have begun. Those not even beginning to do good should not start out by building up what they feel a wholesome love for but by destroying those things with which they wrongly occupy themselves. They do not pursue the untried things they hear of without first perceiving how destructive are the things they have tried. Those unaware of having fallen have no desire to be lifted up, and those who do not feel the pain of a wound do not seek a healing remedy.

We have to begin by showing them how inconsequential are the things they love, and only then should we carefully suggest to them how advantageous are the things they overlook. They must first see that they should shun what they love, and later they will recognize without difficulty that they should love what they shun. They will better accept what they have not tried if they recognize as true the arguments they hear regarding what they have tried. They learn to seek true goods wholeheartedly when they have proven to them how uselessly they have held to what is false.

Let them hear that the good things they are enjoying at present will quickly pass from their enjoyment, while the account to be given of them will remain to punish them without passing away; what pleases them now will be taken from them against their will, and what will pain them hereafter is being reserved for their punishment against their will. Therefore let them have a salutary fear of those things that now bring them harmful pleasure, so that when the sight of the depth of their ruin strikes them, and they perceive how they have arrived at the edge of a precipice, they may retrace their steps; then, as they fear what they had loved they may learn to love what they used to scorn.

Jeremiah was told when he was sent out to preach, "See, today I have set you over nations and kingdoms, to pluck up and to pull down, to destroy and to overthrow, to build and to plant."[1] He could not profitably build up right without first pulling down wrong; without plucking up the thorns of vain love from the hearts of his hearers, his planting of the words of holy preaching in them would have been without effect.

Peter first throws down in order later to build up when, instead of advising the Jews what they were to do, he rebuked them for what they had done: "Jesus of Nazareth, a man attested to you by God by deeds of power, wonders and signs that God did through him among you, as you yourselves know—this man, handed over to you by the definite plan and foreknowledge of God, you crucified and killed by the hands of the wicked. But God raised him up, having freed him from the pains of hell." Overthrown by a recognition of their cruelty, they were intended to seek the upbuilding of holy preaching with uneasiness as great as the profit with which they would listen to it. They replied at once, "What should we do then, men and brothers?" Peter immediately told them, "Repent, and be baptized, every one of you."[2] They would surely have scorned these upbuilding words if they had not first discovered, for their salvation, their downfall and their destruction.

Saul, when light from heaven shone over him, was not at once told the right that he would have to do but the wrong

---

1. Jer. 1:10.
2. Acts 2:22–24, 37–38.

that he had done. After falling to the ground he asked, "Who are you Lord?" and was immediately answered, "I am Jesus of Nazareth, whom you are persecuting." When he went on, "Lord, what will you have me do?" the answer came at once, "Get up and enter the city, and there you will be told what you are to do."[3] You see how the Lord, speaking from heaven, reproved his persecutor's deed, but did not immediately show him what he had to do. You see how the whole structure of his pride had already collapsed to the ground, and how after its ruin he humbly sought to be built up. The words of upbuilding were withheld while his pride was being destroyed. The cruel persecutor was to lie for a time on the ground after his overthrow, and get up more firmly established in goodness for having first fallen, upset completely, from his former error.

Those who have not yet begun to do any good have to have their earlier obstinate wrongdoing overturned by the power of reproof so that they may later be raised up to an attitude of right-doing. We cut down the tall timber of the forest in order to lift it up to the roof of a building, but we do not set it directly into the structure; its greenness is a defect. We must first dry it; the more we draw the moisture out of it below the more securely we can raise it on high.

On the other hand, we must counsel those who do not finish the good they have begun to consider with great circumspection that when they do not fulfill their intention they bring what they began to nothing. If they do not concentrate on moving forward what they evidently must do, even what they have done well moves backward. In this world a human soul is like a boat ascending against the current of a river—it is not allowed to remain in one place because, unless it strives to go higher, it is carried lower. Unless the worker brings the good begun to completion, this abatement itself fights against what has already been done.

3. Acts 9:5–6; 22:6–10.

Solomon says, "One who is loose and slack in work is close kin to a vandal." Those who do not strenuously complete the good they have begun imitate a destroyer's hand by their looseness and negligence. The angel tells the church at Sardis, "Be watchful and strengthen what remains and is on the point of death, for I have not found your works perfect in the sight of my God."[4] Because their works were not found perfect in God's sight, the angel foretold that even those that remained, even those that had been done, were on the point of death. If what is dead in us is not brought back to life, even what we retain as though still alive is destroyed.

We must counsel them to weigh carefully whether not attempting the right way might have been more tolerable than turning back after making the attempt. If they had not looked back, their eagerness to begin would not have weakened into torpor. Let them listen to Scripture: "Not to know the way of righteousness would have been better for them than turning back after knowing it." Let them listen to Scripture: "You are neither cold nor hot. Because you are lukewarm, and neither cold nor hot, I will begin to vomit you out of my mouth."[5]

Those who both undertake and complete good works are hot; those who do not even begin any to be completed are cold. As people pass from cold to hot by way of lukewarm, so do they pass back from hot to cold by way of lukewarm. Those who have lost the cold of unbelief are alive, but unless they pass beyond lukewarmness so as to burn, without any doubt they lose heat, and while they linger in pernicious lukewarmness they are on their way to being cold.

Cold, before becoming lukewarm, is still hopeful, but after the cold comes on, lukewarmness is without hope. Those still in a sinful state do not lose their confidence in

---

4. Prov. 18:9; Rev. 3:2.
5. 2 Pet. 2:21; Rev. 3:15–16.

conversion, but those who have become lukewarm after their conversion have lost the hope that was possible for a sinner. Therefore God seeks those who are either hot or cold to avoid vomiting out the lukewarm. This means that those not yet converted should give hope of conversion, and those already converted should be on fire with the virtues. Otherwise, as they are lukewarm, having returned by their torpor from the hotness they intended to harmful cold, they may be vomited out.

35

People of Reputation

WE MUST COUNSEL DIFFERENTLY those who secretly do wrong and publicly do good, and those who conceal the good they do, yet allow people to think ill of them owing to certain things they do publicly. We must counsel those who secretly do wrong and publicly do good how swiftly human judgments fly past, and how unchangeable and lasting are those of God. We must counsel them to keep their inner eyes fixed on the finish of things because, while the testimony of human applause passes away, the judgment of heaven, which penetrates even to what is concealed, remains in force for an everlasting recompense. When they place their secret wrongs before divine judgment and their right actions before human eyes, the good they do publicly goes unwitnessed while their hidden transgressions do not lack an eternal witness. By hiding their faults from people and displaying their virtues, they both expose what must bring them punishment by their concealment of it, and conceal what could bring them a reward by their exposing it. These people Truth rightly describes as whitewashed tombs, beautiful on the outside, but full of the bones of the dead.[1] They cover the evil of their vices within, while by bringing some of their deeds before human eyes they make a good case for themselves by a mere outward appearance of righteousness.

---

1. Matt. 23:27.

We must counsel them not to underestimate the good they do, but to believe it more deserving than they think; those who reckon human approbation a sufficient reward cheapen their good actions. When they seek transitory applause for a good deed they are selling for a low price something worthy of an eternal recompense. Of the price they receive Truth says, "Truly I tell you, they have received their reward."[2] We must counsel them to consider that when they present themselves in the wrong in secret matters while still putting themselves forward publicly as models for good deeds, they are indicating that we ought to pursue what they avoid, and proclaiming that we should love what they hate. In the end they live to others, and die to themselves.

On the other hand, we must counsel those who secretly do good, yet allow people to think ill of them owing to certain things they do publicly, that while they remain alive by virtue of their right conduct, they are not to kill others by giving them an example of wrong judgment. They are not to love their neighbors less than themselves. When they are drinking wholesome wine, they must not pour out a noxious cup of poison for people intent on observing them. On the one hand, these people contribute little to the lives of their neighbors, and on the other, they oppress them when they strive both to conceal the good they do and to sow evil by the example of certain actions. Those with the ability to crush their desire for praise do harm to upbuilding if they conceal the good they do. A person who shows no works to be imitated is like one who casts seed on the ground and then cuts off the roots as it germinates.

Truth says in the gospel, "Let them see your good works and give glory to your Father in heaven." In the same place, however, he expressed an idea that seems to command something different: "Beware of practicing your righteousness before others in order to be seen by them."[3] What does

---

2. Matt. 6:2 etc.
3. Matt. 5:16; 6:1.

this mean—we are commanded to keep our actions from being seen, and yet they are to be seen—if not that we are to conceal what we do so that we will not be praised, and yet we are to reveal it so that we may increase our heavenly Father's praise?

When the Lord forbids us to practice our righteousness before others he adds, "in order to be seen by them," and when he commands us to let our good deeds be seen by people he adds, "that they may give glory to your Father in heaven." How they should be seen and not seen he shows us by these final phrases—for their own sake doers must not seek to have their deeds seen, and for the sake of their heavenly Father's glory they are not to conceal them.

Frequently a good deed is secret when done publicly, and public when done secretly. Those who seek the glory of their Father above, and not their own, by the good work they do, conceal what they have done from the public, their only witness being the one they are concerned to please. As for those who wish to be observed and praised for good work done in secret, perhaps no one saw what they have displayed, and yet they did it "before others" because they have brought to their good work as many witnesses as the amount of praise their hearts have sought.

When we do not remove the wrong impression of an action—insofar as it is not sinful—from the minds of onlookers, our example provides a fault to all those who think it evil. Frequently those who carelessly allow evil to be imputed to them do nothing wicked personally, and yet they transgress many times over through those who imitate them. That is why Paul says to those who eat certain unclean foods without defiling themselves, but who become a source of scandal and temptation for the immature when they do so, "See that this liberty of yours does not somehow become a stumbling block to the weak," and again, "By your knowledge shall the weak brother or sister for whom Christ died be destroyed? When you sin against your brothers and sisters, and wound their weak consciences, you sin against Christ." That is why Moses, when saying, "You shall not revile the deaf," added immediately, "or put a stumbling block before the blind."[4] To revile the deaf is to disparage someone who is absent and does not hear you; to put a stumbling block before the blind is to do something discreet, but which offers an occasion of stumbling to one who lacks the light of discretion.

4. 1 Cor. 8:9, 11–12; Lev. 19:14.

36

On Exhorting Many

THESE PROCEDURES are what directors of souls should observe in the different phases of their preaching in order to apply the appropriate medicine solicitously to each one's wounds. Great effort is needed in order to meet each person's needs when exhorting them individually, and instructing each one on particular matters with the required attention is very difficult. Far more difficult, however, is counseling, at one and the same time, in a single general exhortation, an audience that is very numerous and dealing with different passions.

We must manage our words with great skill. Even though the vices of our hearers are diverse, we must find something appropriate for each one without contradicting ourselves. Our preaching must pass through the passions in a single stroke, like a two-edged sword, cutting open the tumors of carnal thoughts on either side.

We must preach humility to the proud without increasing fear in the timid, and so impart confidence to the timid that license does not grow stronger in the proud. We must preach responsibility for doing good to the idle and listless without increasing unrestrained and unregulated action in the restless, and we must propose restraint to the restless without leaving the listless and idle untroubled. We must extinguish anger in the impatient without the remiss and easygoing growing more careless, and enkindle zeal in the easygoing without setting the angry on fire. We must inspire the stingy to liberality in giving without relaxing the checks on extravagance in the prodigal, and preach frugality to the prodigal without increasing the hoarding of perishing things by the stingy. We must so praise marriage to the promiscuous that the unmarried are not drawn to lust, and we must so praise physical virginity to the unmarried that the married are not led to despise their fruitful flesh. We must so preach good that we do not unintentionally help evil as well. We must so praise the highest goods as not to despair of the lowest, and so cherish the lowest that they are not considered sufficient with the result that no one aspires to the highest.

37

On Exhorting One Person

THE LABOR OF PREACHERS is difficult when they preach to a general group and have to be attentive to the hidden feelings and interests of each one; as in wrestling, they must turn skillfully from side to side. When, however, they are forced to preach to a single person enslaved to contrary vices, they are worn down by more exhausting labor.

Frequently a person with an exuberant temperament will become excessively depressed when sadness arises suddenly. The preacher must take care to eliminate the sadness that comes occasionally without increasing the exuberance that is a matter of temperament, and to restrain the exuberance that comes from temperament without adding to the sadness, which is occasional.

Other people are burdened with a habit of acting too impulsively, but sometimes a sudden access of fear prevents their doing what they should do quickly. Still others are burdened by a habit of immoderate fear, but sometimes a rash impulse drives them toward what they crave; in the former the sudden access of fear must be suppressed so that their long-cherished impulsiveness does not grow, and in the latter the sudden access of impulsiveness must be repressed so that the fear that comes from their temperament does not gain strength.

What is surprising if the doctors who treat souls observe all these distinctions when those who treat bodies, not hearts, regulate themselves with such skilled discrimination? Often great lethargy oppresses a frail body, and stronger assistance is needed to counteract the lethargy than the frail body will tolerate. Then the doctor strives to take away the supervening disorder without increasing the underlying physical frailty in order that lethargy and life may not end together. He arranges the assistance with such discretion that at one and the same time he counteracts both lethargy and frailty. If medicine for the body, administered singly, can have multiple effects—then is it truly medicine when it is useful against a supervening defect while also preserving the underlying character—why is medicine for the soul, applied in one and the same act of preaching, not capable of countering various kinds of moral disorders? This medicine acts more subtly, inasmuch as it deals with what cannot be seen.

38

Proportionality

IN GENERAL, when a person is attacked by moral weakness resulting from two vices, one presses more lightly and perhaps the other more heavily. In that case we do better to move rapidly against the one that tends more quickly toward death. If preachers cannot keep from causing immediate death without allowing the vice contrary to it to grow, they must tolerate this situation. By skillfully managing their exhortation they should allow the one to grow in order to keep the other from causing immediate death. When they do this they are not aggravating the disease; they are saving the lives of the suffering whom they are treating in order that they can find an appropriate time to seek complete healing.

Those who do nothing to control their gluttony are often goaded by incentives to lust almost to the point of giving in. When they are alarmed by this terrible assault and try to restrain themselves through abstinence, the temptation to vainglory harasses them. In this case they are unable to rid themselves of one vice without promoting another. Which bane should we attack more energetically if not the one that presses more dangerously? We must allow arrogance to grow for a while against the living for the sake of the virtue of abstinence; otherwise lust, resulting from gluttony, might altogether deprive them of life.

Paul, aware that the weak person he was addressing wanted either to continue to do wrong or to enjoy the reward of human approval for doing right, said, "Do you wish to have no fear of authority? Do good, and you will receive its approval."[1] We are not to do good in order to have no fear of authority in this world, or to win in return the glory of transitory praise. When he considered that the weak soul could not reach the degree of strength needed to do without both wrongdoing and praise, the great preacher by his counsel offered something while taking away something else. He made a light concession, and withdrew something more consuming. Because the person could not rise to the point of abandoning all the vices at once, while a familiar one remained the other could be painlessly eliminated.

---

1. Rom. 13:3.

39

Profound Subjects

PREACHERS SHOULD BE AWARE that they must not draw their listeners out beyond their strength. If they do this, the cord of the spirit may be strained too much and snap, if I may put it that way. They must conceal profound subjects from most of their listeners, and scarcely reveal them to a few. Truth himself asks, "Who do you think is the faithful and prudent manager whom the master has set over the household to give them their measure of wheat in due season?"[1] The "measure of wheat" refers to measured words—to give a restricted heart what it cannot contain is to pour this out and waste it.

Paul says, "I could not speak to you as spiritual people, but rather as people of the flesh. As infants in Christ I gave you milk to drink, not solid food." When Moses left his secret conversation with God he veiled his shining face in the presence of the people; he did not make known to the crowd the mysterious glory within.[2]

Through Moses the divine voice commanded that if someone digs a pit and neglects to cover it, and an ox or a donkey falls into it, the person must make restitution.[3] People who arrive at the deep streams of knowledge, and do not cover them before the blunt hearts of their listeners,

---

1. Luke 12:42; cf. Matt. 24:45.
2. 1 Cor. 3:1; Exod. 34:29–35.
3. Exod. 21:33–34.

become liable for punishment if their words cause anyone, clean or unclean, to stumble.

Blessed Job was asked, "Who has given intelligence to the cock?" Holy preachers who cry out in a time of darkness are like cocks crowing in the night, saying, "Now is the time for us to rise from sleep," and, "Awake, you righteous, and sin no more!"[4] Cocks crow loudly in the deepest hours of the night, and as morning approaches their voices become small and thin. Good preachers proclaim plain truths to hearts still in the dark without revealing hidden mysteries; as people approach the light of truth they can hear heaven's more subtle mysteries.

---

4. Job 38:36; Rom. 13:11; 1 Cor. 15:34.

40

Works and Words

A T THIS POINT zeal for love leads me back to what I said above: that preachers must express themselves more in actions than in words. They must lay out a path for those who follow by their good lives rather than indicate a direction by their words.

When the cock the Lord used in his discourse[1] to describe the ideal preacher is ready to crow, it first stretches its wings, and then beats itself with them to make itself more alert. Those who bring forth the word of holy preaching must first be alert and eager to do good; they should not stir up others by their words while they themselves remain inactive. They must stretch themselves by sublime actions, and only then make others solicitous to live good lives. They must beat themselves with the wings of their thoughts, discerning by a serious examination whatever is useless and inert in themselves, and only then amending by severe discipline. Only then ought they to set the lives of others in order by their words. They must first be concerned to punish their own faults by their tears, and then denounce what needs to be punished in others; before they deliver words of exhortation, their deeds should proclaim all that they are about to say.

---

1. Job 38:36.

Epilogue

FREQUENTLY WHEN PREACHING is done appropriately and is fruitful, a secret pleasure over their performance lifts up the hearts of those who do it. They must, then, take care to let fear bite into them. While they treat the wounds of others and recall them to health, they should not swell up through neglect of their own health. They must not abandon themselves in helping their neighbors, or fall while they are lifting others up. Their great virtue has been for some people the occasion of their ruin. Just when they have felt inordinately secure because of their confidence in their own powers they have died unexpectedly through their heedlessness. Virtue struggles with the vices; we flatter ourselves with the pleasure this produces, with the result that those who do good cast off fear and caution and rest secure in their self-confidence. While we are thus inactive the cunning deceiver counts up every good thing we have done and raises us up, swollen with vanity, as if we are superior to everyone else.

The result is that in the eyes of our just judge the recollection of our virtue becomes a pitfall for our spirits. When we recall what we have done, we exalt ourselves in our own eyes, and fall before the source of humility. For this reason the proud are told, "Because you are of surpassing beauty, go down, and sleep with the uncircumcised!" This means, "Because you exalt yourself for the splendor of your virtues, your very beauty will impel you to fall."

Represented by Jerusalem, those taking pride in their virtue are rebuked when they are told, "You were perfect because of my splendor which I had bestowed on you, says the Lord. But you trusted in your beauty, and played the whore because of your fame."[1] We are uplifted by trust in our beauty when we glory within ourselves with a happy assurance concerning what our virtues deserve. This same confidence leads us to play the whore because, when our own thoughts preoccupy and deceive us, evil spirits seduce and corrupt us with countless vices.

We must take note of the words, "you played the whore because of your fame." When we cease to consider our heavenly guide we immediately seek our own praise, and we begin to arrogate to ourselves every good thing we have received to use in heralding our benefactor. We desire to spread our honorable reputation, and we busy ourselves with becoming known and the admiration of all. We play the whore because of our fame when we desert marriage and a lawful bed and prostitute ourselves to a seducing spirit out of our craving for praise. David says, "He delivered their power to captivity, and their beauty to the hand of the foe."[2] Power is delivered to captivity and beauty to the hand of the foe when the ancient enemy masters those deceived by their pride in doing good.

This pride in their virtue frequently tempts even the chosen in some way or other, although without fully overcoming them. When exalted, they are left to themselves, and when left to themselves they are reduced to fear. David, again, says, "I said in my prosperity, 'I shall never be moved.'" But because he had become conceited from trusting in his virtue he soon adds what he endured: "You turned your face away from me, and I became troubled." He means, "I believed I was strong among my virtues, but when I was abandoned I came to realize how great my weakness is." Again, he says, "I have sworn and have determined to observe your righteous ordinances."

---

1. Ezek. 32:19; 16:14–15.
2. Ps. 78:61.

But because continuing to observe what he had sworn was not within his power he was troubled and at once discovered his own weakness. He had immediate recourse to the help of prayer, saying, "I have been humbled on every side, Lord; give me life according to your word."[3]

Sometimes divine guidance, before moving us forward by its gifts, recalls to our minds the memory of our own weakness so that we will not become conceited owing to the virtues we have received. So the prophet Ezekiel, as often as he is summoned to contemplate heavenly realities, is first called "son of man."[4] The Lord is, as it were, openly counseling him, saying, "So that you will not exalt your heart in pride because of what you see, weigh carefully what you are. While penetrating the highest realities you must be aware that you are a human being; while being rapt beyond yourself you must be alarmed and recalled to yourself by the restraints of your own weakness."

Hence, when we are flattered by the abundance of our virtues we must direct our inner eyes to our frailty, and we must humble ourselves in a wholesome way. We should not regard the good we have done, but rather what we have neglected to do. Then, when our hearts are crushed by recollection of our frailty, we may be confirmed more strongly in virtue in the presence of the source of humility.

Frequently almighty God, although perfecting in large part those who guide others, leaves them in some small part imperfect. Then, even as they are resplendent with marvelous virtues, they may pine away with disgust at their own imperfection. While they toil on, struggling against little things, they do not exalt themselves because of the great. As they are not strong enough to overcome their smallest weaknesses, they do not dare to take pride in their outstanding accomplishments.

---

3. Ps. 30:6, 7; 119:106, 107.
4. Ezek. 2:1 etc.